Conversations Over the Airwaves

Conversations Over the Airwaves

and the deception transmissions that hoodwinked the enemy

The extraordinary life of Major
Rowland 'Rowley' Shears, BEM, TD, G8KW

Richard Shears

THE CHOIR PRESS

Copyright © 2025 Richard Shears

All rights reserved. No part of this publication may be reproduced or transmitted in any form or by any means, electronic or mechanical including photocopying, recording or any information storage or retrieval system, without prior permission in writing from the publishers.

The right of Richard Shears to be identified as the author of this work has been asserted by him in accordance with the Copyright, Designs and Patents Act 1988

First published in the United Kingdom in 2025 by

The Choir Press

ISBN 978-1-78963-538-6

This book is dedicated to my father who decided to write down his stories so that they could be shared.

PICTURE ACKNOWLEDGEMENTS:

Front cover, Morse Code image and Egypt map – courtesy Shutterstock Images

Luftwaffe Target Map and Brooklands site damage – courtesy Brooklands Museum

No. 5 HP Wireless set and B2 spyset – courtesy Louis Meulstee, (www.wftw.nl)

Maps – initially created with Mapchart (www.mapchart.net)

The G8KW Trophy – courtesy DARC

KW Vanguard front panel and inside – KW Electronics Ltd leaflet, reprinted from Short Wave Magazine, March 1958

All other images/photographs are from the author's personal collection.

Contents

Author's Introduction ix

Part I – INTRODUCTION AND EARLY YEARS

1 Family Background 2
2 School Years 3
3 The Start of Working Life 6

Part II – ROWLEY'S WAR

4 The Start of World War II and Journey to the Middle East 11
5 Early Days in the Middle East 19
6 The War Impact Back Home in 1940 21
7 Polygon Wireless Station (Abbassieh, Cairo) 29
8 Panzer Tanks on the Russian Front and the Official Secrets Act 35
9 The Deception Game Begins 38
10 Preparing to Contact the Enemy 42
11 Assuming a New Identity for Operation Cheese 45
12 A Padded Cell and the Hunt for an Understudy! 50
13 More Portions of Cheese and a Commission 52
14 We Need More Funds… 56
15 A Trainee for the Cheese Team 59
16 Improving Desert Communications at Polygon Wireless Station 61
17 JCJC Broadcasting Services for the Troops in Egypt (1942–1944) 68
18 Prizes for Deception 76
19 'A' Force Cairo 79
20 Operation Wild Goose – A New German Agent 81
21 The Gezira Project – the Spy and the Sabotage Expert 92
22 Back to Cheese in Advance of the Battle for El Alamein 102
23 Post Battle of El Alamein and into 1943 104

24	Mentioned in Despatches and British Empire Medal	106
25	1944 Undercover in Crete (May) and Task Force to Athens (October)	112

Part III – POST-WAR GERMANY

26	Military Life Continues in 1945	123
27	1945: Journey to Germany – The Long Arm of Coincidence	125
28	Back to Broadcasting at Langenberg, Germany	129
29	Police Radio Network – Hamburg, Germany (1946–1947)	131
30	The Control Commission for Germany	133
31	The First Train into Berlin at the End of the Russian Blockade (May 12th 1949)	135
32	Final Days in Frankfurt, Germany	145
33	Working with the German Radio Amateurs (1946–1950)	146

Part IV – BACK IN THE UK and THE KW STORY

34	Working in the UK	152
35	Establishing the KW Brand	153
36	Some Other KW Highlights	165
	KW Equipment Plays a Starring Role	165
	Working with the Pirates – (Britain's Pirate Radio Stations)	165
	British Trans-Arctic Expedition (BTA)	167
	A Temporary End to the Original KW Brand and New Start-ups	168
	KW Remembered	169

Part V – OTHER MEMORIES OF MY FATHER

37	Family Life and On the Airwaves	172
38	Postscript Regarding His War Years	175
GLOSSARY		176

Author's Introduction

This biography of my father, Rowland George Shears (1919–2009), known by all as Rowley, is based on a collection of his personal notes and letters which he collated in the 1990s when he intended to write his autobiography. It's his own story based on his recollections and is centred on the world of radio communications. His early hobby, fascination and commitment to radio communications shaped his wartime military service, and his remarkable experiences during that timeframe form the major part of his written accounts, and this book. The book covers Rowley's early days as an amateur radio enthusiast, his military career from 1939 to 1947 (Middle East, Crete, Athens and post-World War II Germany) and subsequent civilian work for the Foreign Office, in Germany, until 1950. To complete his life story, a short summary of his life post-1950 has been included at the end of the book.

The start of Rowley's memoir writing was a significant moment for the family. In common with so many World War II (WWII) military personnel he had never previously talked in much detail about his war exploits, ever mindful of the secretive nature of the work he did and the fact that he had signed the Official Secrets Act in 1941 when he started working for SIME (Security Intelligence Middle East). That organisation, which was created and based in Cairo from 1939, was a mainly military body acting as the local arm of the Security Service MI5 and had links to all the other British intelligence and security services. With a responsibility for tracking down enemy agents in the Middle East, SIME utilised the services of turned agents to spread disinformation over the airwaves and to deceive the German military intelligence service (Abwehr).

Rowley was, by nature, a very outgoing person with a strong sense of humour who enjoyed socialising and liked to relay amusing facts and anecdotes to an audience. Once he had begun his autobiography work, family dinner table conversations were peppered with anecdotes about his experiences and the people he had met during his time in the Middle East, Greece and Germany, during and just after WWII. The origin of the fictitious *Paul Nicosoff* was one of many familiar stories that he shared with the family. Sometimes he referred to himself, in a jokey way, as the "big Cheese" but didn't really elaborate any further about this. We never fully understood the meaning behind this reference until later when we read his notes, and other stories about the Cheese Network began to emerge, following de-classification of secret files.

Sadly, Rowley's memoir writing task was never completed as he stopped writing when he began suffering the effects of Alzheimer's. Fortunately, what he had already documented, or recollected, about his early career provided a good starting point for this book about his life. Despite the Alzheimer's, Rowley retained very clear recollections of the significant events and occasions from his wartime and post-war experiences up till the end of his life.

As this book is primarily based on Rowley's notes, the accounts and recollections in this book may deviate from other published resources. Much has been written elsewhere about the same timeline in the Middle East, the work of SIME and the skilled work of those who were instrumental in providing misleading information to the German Abwehr (the German military intelligence service) via invented agents such as 'Paul Nicosoff'. Readers of this book can draw their own conclusions on how this might fit in with Rowley's stories which are based on his personal memories rather than any official sources.

Although colleagues' names are mentioned in Rowley's recollections, he did not specifically mention the name of Nicosoff and the names of agents, such as Alex, whose Morse style he imitated and whose identity he took on in 1941, would have been aliases or code names.

Rowley's meetings with agents like 'Alex', who were managed by SIME, were probably kept deliberately brief and it's unlikely that the senior intelligence officers shared much detail with him in the early days. Although the officers were very grateful for his competence and skills in radio communications, Rowley was a very young and non-commissioned junior rank when he started working with SIME at the age of 22, in early 1941. He was later commissioned in 1943.

I would like to thank my cousin, and family historian, Colin Durack for his research on the Shears family history which I have included in this book. He also kindly shared his earlier writings, based on Rowley's written notes and conversations with my father, which he had used as a basis for many talks over the years.

I would also like to thank my wife, Anne, for her help, support, and valuable suggestions during the development of this book. She carefully went through all of Rowley's handwritten notes and letters to ensure accuracy on timelines and stories, and acted as 'editor in chief'.

Richard Shears

Part I
INTRODUCTION AND EARLY YEARS

Chapter One
Family Background

My father, Rowland George Shears, was born on the 4th September 1919 in New Barnet, Hertfordshire (now a London borough) and was always known as Rowley, probably to avoid confusion as his father had the similar first name of Roland. Roland Hallam Shears was a motor & cycle engineer as well as being a 1st Team player with Barnet Football Club when they won the London League in 1909–1910. Rowley's mother was Dorothy Victoria Shears (née Ratcliff). Rowley was the eldest of three children and had two younger sisters, Dorothy (Colin Durack's mother) and Ruth.

One interesting ancestor of note was John Hallam, one of Rowley's great-grandfathers on his father's side. He was a saddler by trade and was born during 1817 in Leicester. In later life, John Hallam became a Master Drummer and Colour Sergeant in the 17th Regiment of Foot and Rifle Brigade of The Royal Leicester Regiment. He served in the Army for over twenty-one years and was in Ireland as well as overseas on the Crimean Peninsula as part of the 13th Prince Albert's Light Infantry of 1855. Following that conflict, John was duly awarded the Crimean Medal plus clasp for the taking of Sevastopol on 25th November 1855, which resulted in the subsequent defeat of the Russian armies.

Interestingly the family name of Hallam has been passed down through the generations, not only to Rowley's father but also to myself and to my younger brother.

Chapter 2

School Years

Rowley stayed in New Barnet whilst growing up and was educated locally in Barnet at the Secondary School and the Technical School. At a young age, he developed a passion for all things mechanical and electrical, including cars and trains, and wanted to become a pilot. He avidly followed the exploits of all the great innovators of the 1920s and 1930s. In particular, he followed the achievements of Sir Nigel Gresley, (the Chief Mechanical Engineer of the LNER) who was the designer of the famous steam locomotives The Flying Scotsman and The Mallard. Perhaps the fact that these locomotives regularly passed the bottom of the family garden in New Barnet, and that Gresley himself was a resident in nearby Hadley Wood, then later Salisbury Hall near St. Albans, encouraged his interest in him.

Rowley's early passion and enthusiasm for radio communications was greatly encouraged and influenced by his father who owned an amateur radio set. Rowley had fond early memories of his father using the radio. He remembered the very long length of wire for an aerial, the bright emitter valves (tubes) and basket weave coils as well as the sound of a foreign language over the airwaves from the Eiffel tower transmitter.

Rowley assembled his first radio from a kit produced by Scott-Taggart (the ST300) after early experimentations with creating wired-up miniature radios in matchboxes. The new possibilities of communication over vast distances really caught his imagination in the late 1920s and early 1930s so his next project was assembling a Lissen 'Skyscraper' kit. He was then able to receive British Empire Service broadcasts on several wavelengths along with numerous short-wave broadcasts from Holland, Germany, France and Sweden. Inspired by the magazine Popular Wireless, which was delivered to his home by the local newsagent, he also studied the science of radio waves to further his knowledge. He was fascinated by all the broadcasts and different music that he picked up from around the world and admitted that from then on, his main interest in life was listening to radio stations worldwide.

In 1934 he constructed, from spare parts, his first four-valve short-wave receiver and erected aerials and antennae on a 60-foot pole in the family garden. He said that the big event of the week for him was to tune in to a broadcast from Melbourne, before 2pm UK time, to hear the interval signal (the sound of the Kookaburra bird) followed by the chimes of the Melbourne Post Office clock. Other favourites were the Dutch overseas broadcast "the friendly voice of the Netherlands" and the good signal from KDKA Pittsburgh from which he heard "Brylcreem, Brylcreem" over the radio. The following year a friend of his father was so impressed by the results of this short-wave receiver that he offered to buy it for £20, which was a lot of money in those days. His father's friend was apparently still using it when war broke out!

Rowley had wide interests in music when he was young. He remembered camping in his back garden with friends during the summer holidays and listened to Quito, Ecuador and other South American stations which broadcasted rumba and tango music. His mother, noting his interest in music, tried to encourage him to play the piano and after buying him one she arranged for him to have lessons every Friday after school.

Following on from the success of his first short wave receiver, Rowley built himself another one, this time with six valves, and in late 1934, aged fifteen, he joined the Radio Society of Great Britain (RSGB) as an associate member. He was issued with his British Receiving Station membership number, BRS1904.

Recognising that Rowley was so absorbed in his radio interests, his mother agreed that he could give up his piano lessons and learn Morse code instead. Rowley noted that it was this decision that proved so beneficial to him later. Rowley was taught by some experienced radio hams at Southgate Radio Club, namely G6QI (Richard Walker) and 2BKR (Frank Appleton) and soon became fully proficient in the use and understanding of Morse. He was then able to pass the tests for sending and receiving Morse code which were held at Barnet Post Office. Rowley notes that at this time telegrams were sent and received via skilled Morse operators employed at most main Post Offices, branches of British General Post Office (GPO), so this is why the tests were held there.

After passing the tests and the written theory examinations covering all aspects of radio transmission and receiving, he was able to apply to the Postmaster General at the GPO for a transmitting licence, at a cost of ten shillings. As he was under 16 years of age the licence had to be issued in his father's name which, he was advised, would continue until he reached the age of 21. In 1935, Rowley was issued with an 'artificial aerial' licence with the callsign 2BXL. After twelve months of conducting and recording findings on various experiments on transmitter designs using the artificial aerial, he submitted a report on his findings to the Postmaster General and, as a result, was invited to apply for a full transmitting licence with a choice of callsign. The Postmaster General suggested that Rowley might like to apply for one of the new 'G8' prefixes, so he requested either G8RS or G8KW. Rowley then chose the latter and noted that, as he was at an impressionable age, the 'KW' clearly suggested a 'power-house' with a copious amount of electrical power. The 'KW' became synonymous with Rowley's work in later life. A picture of the first G8KW licence issued to Rowley is shown in the photos section.

Chapter 3
The Start of Working Life

At the age of sixteen, Rowley thought about leaving school, even though his school housemaster had advised that he could qualify for university. Rowley accepted the offer of a one-year apprenticeship on valve development in a laboratory at Cosmos Lamps in Enfield in Middlesex (now a London borough). He would cycle to work, leaving home at 6.15 each morning, six days a week, for a 7.30am start. He was assisting the Chief Engineer in developing new mini-valves which later became known as 'acorn' valves due to their shape. Rowley notes that at this time there was a requirement by the armed forces to develop communications equipment which would operate over higher frequencies. The new 'acorn' valve design allowed the Hallicrafter company, originally a leading American amateur radio equipment producer, to create a new military communications receiver for bands 30-150 MHz (megahertz) which was in production by 1939 and widely used during World War II (WWII).

Although Rowley found the work at Cosmos extremely interesting, he commented that he found the long cycling journey to Enfield rather tiring so was delighted when, in 1936, another radio ham (T.L. Franklin, G5HO) offered him a job at Invicta Radio & Television (part of Pye Radio Limited). The job was at their Ever-Ready factory in Holloway, North London. He jumped at it as it meant he could travel by train from New Barnet station to Finsbury Park, followed by a short bus ride. On the train journey back to New Barnet from London he regularly met up with G6QI (Richard Walker) where they talked about transmitters and aerial designs.

The job at Invicta was in the test department where he was designing equipment for testing the new TV receivers that Invicta were manufacturing in the very early days of television. He gained considerable technical knowledge during this time and, with the permission of the General Manager (T.L. Franklin), he was able to use the facilities of the sheet metal shop where he constructed numerous metal chassis, panels and a 6-foot-high rack housing to contain his power supply, modulator and transmitter radio equipment. This allowed Rowley to move away from his earlier 'bread board' designs to something more professional. Rowley notes that the equipment was removed (impounded) and interned by the Post Office at the start of the war and that the 'Mullard' output valve (type TZ05/20) was later removed and used "for the war effort" in 1941. At this time, Rowley was sent a letter from the Incorporated Radio Society of Great Britain (RSGB) on behalf of the Wireless Telegraphy Board, which urgently appealed for donations, or sale, of all types of instruments which were required by the Navy, Army and Air Force for training purposes. Examples of equipment needed for the war effort included Avometers, moving coil meters, oscilloscopes, oscillators and monitor cathode ray tubes (CRTs). Rowley received compensation for the Mullard valve and kept the original documentation relating to this. Both the RSGB appeal letter and the compensation letter are pictured in the photos section.

On his seventeenth birthday in 1936, Rowley took, and passed, his driving test in Hertford. He drove there himself in his father's 1932 Morris Minor 2-seater. However, it was not until March 1939 that he was able to purchase a car for himself. This was a second-hand 1932 Hillman Minx saloon with the registration VK 7566, for which he paid £27.

Whilst employed at Invicta, war clouds were gathering and Rowley realised that, should conscription be introduced, he would be in the first age group to be called up and would have no choice of Service, Regiment or Corps. Keen to have some choice in the matter, Rowley proactively sought enlistment in the Territorial Army, Royal Corps of Signals. A friend of Rowley's, who worked locally for Standard Telephones and Cables Ltd at New Southgate, told him that there was a Territorial Signals Company established there, which was only four miles from his home. He made some enquiries and during the short interview he mentioned that his normal Morse speed was 25 words per minute, sending and receiving, (against a 12 words per minute standard required for amateur radio transmitting licences). On hearing this, Captain Baker, the Officer Commanding (who was also an executive at Standard Telephones & Cables in central London) presented Rowley with an enlistment document for signature and gave him his "Kings Shilling"[1]. Rowley was the only member of that unit not working for Standard Telephones & Cables Ltd (STC). Rowley noted how much he enjoyed the weekend signals training as well as the 2-week summer camps in August 1938 and 1939 at Dibgate Camp in Folkestone, the last one being held only two weeks before war was declared.

Rowley's enthusiasm for radio transmitting experiments got him into trouble on one occasion in 1938 when the GPO Engineer in Chief's Office (radio branch) wrote to advise him that his call sign was detected operating on a frequency outside of the authorised 7 megacycles[2] (7 mc/s) bandwidth, which was considered an infringement of his licence. Rowley's very full reply explained that at the time, he was operating on an allowed bandwidth but had experienced "harmonics" which he believed might have caused the irregularity. Rowley further explained that the signal detected by the GPO was probably a "harmonic of the fundamental frequency" whilst he was experimenting with his aerial systems. He had become aware of the problem before he had received their letter and had now resolved it. The GPO authority accepted his explanation and his assurances that "he would endeavour to avoid a further occurrence" of this issue.

---

[1] King's Shilling – Historical term meaning to agree to serve in the British Army or Royal Navy.

[2] Megacycles – short for megacycles per second (mc/s) in use at the time. Unit of frequency, denoting one million cycles per second. Now replaced by megahertz, MHz.

In the summer of 1939, the War Office approached the RSGB to find radio amateurs (radio hams) who would be prepared to monitor and intercept enemy Morse code signals on short wave bands, emanating from within Britain and being sent to Germany. MI5 (the British Security Service) were setting up a specialist unit, to be known as the Radio Security Service (RSS) and several of Rowley's radio contacts were recruited to the unit as Voluntary Interceptors (VIs). These VIs operated from their homes using their own radio receivers and reported on what they heard.

Part II
ROWLEY'S WAR

Chapter 4
The Start of World War II and Journey to the Middle East

On 1st September 1939, two days before war was declared and three days before his 20th birthday, Rowley was "called to the Colours"[1] as a Signalman and told to report to J section No. 3 Company (44th Division), Royal Corps of Signals, at STC New Southgate. The Signals group quickly collected their arms equipment and vehicles, some of which were old '3-tonners', probably of World War I (WWI) vintage, with canvas front wind breaks instead of glass windscreens. Rowley notes that within the STC factory grounds they all formed into a column before heading to Sevenoaks in Kent, near to where he later lived, to commence their initial training.

When he arrived in Sevenoaks, arrangements were in place to requisition the Odeon theatre car park, a school, several halls and private residences as well as the Conservative office (which was to become the Company office). He slept on the floorboards of a house which had been requisitioned near to the Post Office. He recalled a night when he was on guard duty at the entrance to the Odeon car park in Sevenoaks, which turned out to be the only time that he undertook guard duty in his entire Army career! During this time Rowley was granted a trade rating of Operator Wireless and Line Class 3 which meant extra pay. Later, when he was in the Middle East, he qualified for Wireless Operator and Line Class 1, Electrician Signals Class 1 and Despatch Rider Class 3.

In November 1939, No. 3 Company moved to Misterton, a small village in Somerset, and when his division received orders to proceed to France, as part of the BEF (British Expeditionary Force),

---
[1] Called to Colours – an order to serve in the Armed Forces.

Rowley was instructed to go elsewhere. He was transferred to 12th Division Signals at their Chiswick base in West London. Here, he was made an instructor in Morse, electricity and magnetism and the workings of different transmitters and receivers, including the quite old 'No. 1' sets. He was promoted from Signalman to the rank of Lance Corporal and was pleased that this allowed him to visit his parents on a number of weekends in November and December 1939. Rowley ran two classes over the next two to three months – one for beginners to Morse and another for those who had already reached speeds of 5-8 words per minute (wpm). He was tasked with improving Morse for both groups to levels of 10-12 wpm and 15 wpm respectively, by March 1940. His classes were also tutored by another Corporal on 'Morse by sight' using Aldis Lamps[1] and flags.

His promotion to Lance Corporal was formerly confirmed on the 15th March 1940 and in recognition of his success as a Morse trainer and his thorough knowledge of the workings of the No. 1 transmitter and receiver sets, his Commanding Officer (CO) called him for an interview and asked if he had considered applying for a commission. The CO offered to recommend him for a six-month course at the Officer Cadet Training Unit (OCTU) in either Aldershot or Catterick. Rowley declined the offer as he wanted to gain more practical experience in the ranks on active service with the company. Rowley's CO told him that he had made a "commendable decision" and was sure the opportunity would arise again in the future.

At the end of March, rumours had been circulating about their impending move overseas and as tropical kit had been seen in the divisional stores this suggested they would soon be bound for India or the Far East. A few weeks after his interview with the CO the unit received movement orders and Rowley was soon heading north on the Euston to Glasgow train line. There was speculation that they would all embark at Greenock on the Clyde, but they ended up at

---

[1] Aldis Lamp – a visual signalling device to transmit messages in Morse code.

Gailes Camp (between Troon and Irvine) for a while, sleeping under canvas. After a couple of weeks, they went to Liverpool and camped out under canvas on Aintree Racecourse, ready for embarkation on 25th June 1940. This happened to be the same day that France surrendered. Rowley notes the long march to the Warwick Street Barracks in Liverpool, made more memorable by the "kindness" of the residents of Scotland Road who rushed out of their houses with mugs of tea, bottles of lemonade and beer and wished them luck. He remembers one old lady, pressing a sixpence into his hands, whilst saying "Good luck son, God bless you, safe return".

After a week or so at the barracks, Rowley joined the *RMS Mauretania*, which was a brand-new ship built by the Cunard White Star Line for the Atlantic run and had been launched from Liverpool in 1938. She had been requisitioned by the British Government, converted into a troop ship and was now painted in battleship grey and armed with new guns. Rowley commented that the Cunard captain and staff had been retained, and everything was brand new and very comfortable.

Sailing out of Liverpool when it was dark at about 9pm in June 1940, the *Mauretania* was escorted by a Royal Navy cruiser and a frigate. Rowley explains that the ship received news reports through the radio officers on board and after about 36 hours of sailing a special message was broadcast over the ship's Tannoy, which had up until then only been used to relay information about ship safety, deck drills and exercises. The special announcement was that the British traitor, known as Lord Haw-Haw (real name William Joyce), had broadcast that the *RMS Mauretania*, which had recently sailed from Liverpool, had been sunk by a U-boat in the Irish Sea with the loss of thousands of lives. Thankfully all was OK on the *Mauretania* and Rowley realised that there must have been spies around Liverpool or Merseyside passing information back to Germany, possibly by radio. Rowley notes that the "Germany Calling" propaganda radio programme was broadcast from a transmitter overlooking the North Sea near the Dutch border to ensure that a strong signal was heard in London and the South East as well as the Birmingham area.

The *Mauretania* was soon joined by the *RMS Queen Mary* and *RMS Aquitania* with its four huge funnels. The convoy, carrying thousands of troops, was completed by a group of other escort ships which varied in number. Rowley remarked that sometimes they all advanced in line abreast of each other and other times they were in a column. It became a habit every morning to go up on deck and check if the other ships were still with them even though no one on board knew where they were heading.

After crossing the equator on 10th July 1940, the fully escorted convoy called at Freetown, Sierra Leone, where they weren't allowed to go ashore. When they left Sierra Leone with their two companion ships their escort changed to *HMAS Sydney*. The *Mauretania* arrived in Cape Town late July 1940, and Rowley learned that they had taken a large detour towards the coast of Brazil to avoid U-boats in the Atlantic, prior to arriving there.

In his memoirs, Rowley recounts, in detail, the very warm welcome he received in Cape Town. Soon after docking, the troops were allowed to go ashore to a tremendous welcome. He was told by the locals that they were the first British troops to arrive in their town since WWI. During the morning, he went with a friend to the post office to buy stamps and to send a few cards home. Whilst waiting at the counter to be served, a charming lady, whom Rowley thought to be in her early sixties, asked them if they would like to be shown around Cape Town in her car. Rowley and his friend graciously accepted and all three drove off in her Austin 12 Tourer. It was mid-winter there but wonderfully sunny and their charming hostess had already folded back the canvas roof. They had excellent views of the buildings she pointed out before driving eastwards and then along the coast to where the Indian Ocean meets with the Atlantic. She then drove to a nearby beach whereupon she produced a hamper from the rear boot of the car. Seated at the picnic table they enjoyed the sandwiches and cakes she had so generously packed. This was followed by some old-fashioned ginger beer poured from a stone bottle.

Their hostess asked a variety of questions about their activities back home and how people in the UK were managing. They learned that she had lived in many places in England, Scotland and Wales. After lunch she drove them inland to a wine estate and they were shown one of the old-style Dutch mansions. They were also taken on a quick trip to the top of Table Mountain which, fortunately, did not have the well-known 'tablecloth' cloud formation over it. Reaching the foot of the mountain, on the approach to the town, she invited them to her house for a cup of tea and "Queenie cakes" (a small sultana cake) before she drove Rowley and his friend back to the ship. On entering the hostess's home, Rowley had realised that this kind lady was the wife of the Bishop of Cape Town. Unfortunately, the Bishop was away in Elizabethville attending a conference and Rowley was very disappointed not to be able to meet him.

Once back on-board ship (in time for the evening meal) Rowley was immediately aware of an atmosphere of excitement and animation. He listened to his shipmates talk about their day, which had been completely different to his. Theirs was full of dancehalls, cabarets, dancing girls and pubs, quite different to that enjoyed by Rowley and his friend. Rowley comments that everyone had enjoyed their visit to Cape Town, there were no arrests by the Military Police, and they all felt proud to be British.

After Cape Town they sailed just a few miles around the coast to the Naval Base at Simonstown where the refuelling and victualling were carried out, before going on to Colombo, Ceylon. Rowley notes that he guessed it was Colombo for above the port warehouses was a structure with enormous letters which read "CEYLON FOR GOOD TEA". Here, in Colombo, part of the Forces contingent, including Rowley's Signals Company, disembarked and were taken to an Army barracks. They learnt that the *RMS Mauretania* carried on to Singapore, delivering the troops that would later fight the

Japanese there before surrendering to them and suffering terrible treatment at their captors' hands. After a few days, and a bit of local food shopping, Rowley joined an old, much smaller, P&O liner, which had probably been brought out of retirement, and sailed to Bombay. Rowley notes that they experienced rough seas on the journey and when arriving in Bombay, learned that an even older P&O liner in their convoy had been carrying live cattle for the purpose of feeding the troops and crews. The effect of the high seas had made most of the cattle sea-sick!

After a week's stopover in Bombay they became aware that their destination was to be the Middle East. Rowley and his company joined HM Troop carrier *Dilwarra*, a purpose-built ship which had left Liverpool for her maiden voyage six months earlier. Rowley notes that she was very comfortable and "sailed well".

Soon after leaving port Rowley was instructed to report to the Radio Room on the upper deck. Passing a sign which read 'Out of Bounds to Troops', he knocked on the Radio Room door and went inside. He met two Merchant Marine radio officers who introduced themselves and explained that they were one officer short due to having to leave him in a military hospital in Bombay for treatment. The senior officer said he understood that Rowley was a good Morse operator and so he would be working in 4-hour shifts with them. He would be listening only and otherwise observing 'radio silence' unless there was an emergency, and they were instructed by the Captain "to send a message". It was explained to Rowley that enemy naval vessels and U-boats had equipment on board that could pinpoint their position to within 50 miles even if they sent just a few dots and dashes. Rowley was to take messages from the Admiralty (in cipher) as well as news bulletins in plain language (sent from Rugby, England), which would then be typed up for display on the ship's notice board. All the messages were received in Morse at 25 wpm, which Rowley was comfortable with.

Rowley noted that he couldn't believe his luck, as he had a bunk in a cabin next to the Radio Room, whilst other troops had to endure temperatures above 38 degrees Celsius 'down below' from around mid-day and through the afternoon with only a few degrees cooler at night. When on duty he had tea, food and cool drinks brought to him as well as an occasional beer or gin and tonic from the Officers Mess. Rowley comments that he had never tried gin and tonic before, only the odd port and lemon!

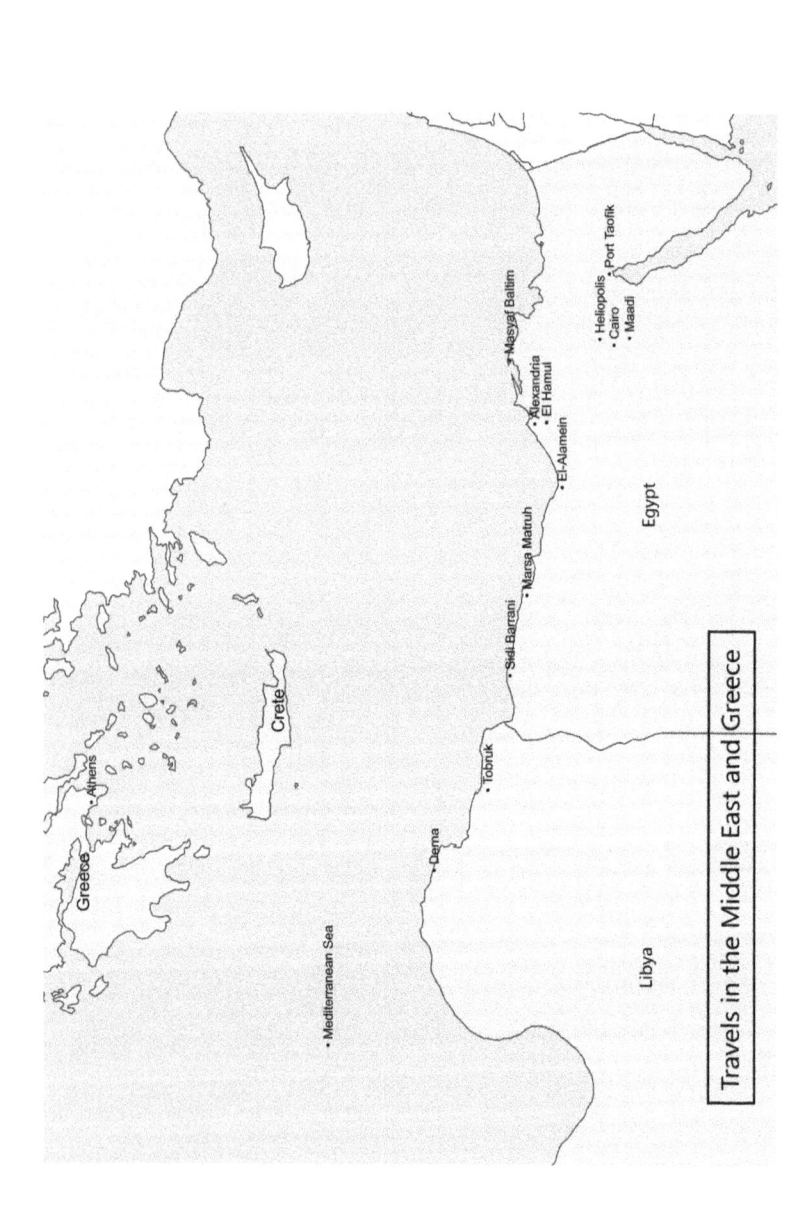

Travels in the Middle East and Greece

Chapter 5
Early Days in the Middle East

On 23rd August 1940, Rowley disembarked at Port Tawfiq (Taofik), at the southern end of the Suez Canal, in Egypt. The journey from Liverpool had taken almost two months and fortunately they did not experience any enemy action on the way.

Rowley and his company marched towards a waiting train which was being driven by the Corps of Royal Engineers. The railway carriages were from Egyptian State Railways and had open windows with no glass, so they endured a very long hot journey across miles and miles of desert as smoke from the engine blew into the carriages. They caught occasional glimpses of the Pyramids and Cairo landmarks then drove through the suburbs of Cairo and out the other side to Diglah camp at Maadi. Here, Rowley was based under canvas for the next six weeks. He recalls he was allowed occasional visits into Cairo by train and notes that he visited the Sphinx and the Pyramids with a friend and was able to climb to the top of the Cheops Pyramid and have a guided tour of the interior passages and chambers. Whilst enjoying the sights of Cairo, the Dunkirk evacuation of troops and the Luftwaffe bombing of London, and other cities back home, seemed a long way away but always stayed in their minds.

As soon as he was established at the camp, Rowley was giving Morse lessons in a marquee to signalmen in groups of up to twenty. Within a week he was given details by his Officer Commanding (OC) to "set up a security radio net" with other local bases, using their old No. 1 radio sets. The No. 1 set was a portable transmitter/receiver, developed in 1933, for 'short range' use. This special communications network had been authorised to use four specific frequencies for an exercise to determine the best and most reliable frequencies to be used over a 24-hour period between Diglah (as Control Station), GHQ Cairo, Abbassieh, Kasn-nil barracks and Mena camp. Whilst Rowley was put in charge, he was allocated other non-commissioned officers (NCOs) to drive to the other locations with their equipment. He drew up a test schedule, for both speech and Morse transmission, and each NCO was told to record the results. This resulted in all four 'out stations' being able to contact the base station as well as each other.

On one afternoon whilst busy working out the schedules for the tests to continue through the night, a "runner" from the orderly room appeared with a note from the Company Sergeant Major (CSM) ordering Rowley to attend guard duties at 18.00 hours that evening. Rowley asked the runner to inform the CSM that he had been excused guard duties by his Captain (Moncrieff), as he was on "special duties". A few minutes later the orderly returned along with the angry CSM and, before Rowley could explain fully about the importance of his 'security wireless net' work, he was put on a charge. After Rowley did get the chance to explain his work, a rather enraged CSM immediately headed off to speak with the Captain and nothing further was heard about the incident! The 'wireless net' worked well and became a permanent feature in case air raids disrupted telephone cables in and around Cairo.

Chapter 6
The War Impact Back Home in 1940

Rowley reached his 21st birthday on 4th September 1940. We don't know if he had a chance to celebrate in any way on that day, but it turned out to be a sad day for other members of his family back home.

Rowley had a cousin back in England who was helping with the war effort at the Vickers-Armstrongs aircraft factory at Brooklands in Weybridge, Surrey, having started out originally as an apprentice in the factory. The cousin was called William Arthur George Philbin but was known in the family as "Little Billy" to differentiate from his father of the same name. He was 20 years old and lived a few miles away in Chertsey Road, Shepperton.

According to Brooklands records, as well as various local newspaper reports from the time, there were a large number of factory units around the Brooklands site where Vickers were producing the Wellington bombers and Hawkers, the renowned Hurricane fighter planes. The staff at the site were always aware of the threat of attack from the Luftwaffe and there had been a small number of attempts in July and August of 1940 as the Battle of Britain was raging.

The factories and racetrack were camouflaged by netting to avoid recognition from the air but the main railway line running alongside the site could not be hidden. There were no barrage balloons (a deterrent to low aircraft attacks) installed at this time. The Luftwaffe were apparently well aware of the site as can be seen on a map of the area, obtained by Brooklands after the war and reproduced in the photos section of this book.

On 4th September, around 100 aircraft from specialist German bombing units left their bases in Northern France to make simultaneous attacks on different aircraft manufacturing sites in the UK, as part of an attempt to destroy the RAF. Brooklands was one of their targets.

One group of the 100 aircraft, comprising 13 Messerschmitt Bf 110 Luftwaffe fighter-bombers, each carrying 2 x 500kg bombs, was heading towards the factories at Brooklands, before splitting into two groups. The bombers dived in two waves, each from opposing directions, and dropped their bombs on the Vickers factory. Sadly, there was no early warning of the raid and although an alarm was raised it was too late for local defences to take any action. This raid took place at 13.24 hrs just as the factory lunchtime was ending and before the start of the afternoon shift. It lasted for only three minutes but the bombs caused much damage to, and around, the machine shop, wing shop and repair shop as well as to large amounts of roof glazing. As a result of the raid 88 people, including Rowley's cousin "Little Billy", lost their lives and over 400 others were injured.

Amazingly, Wellington aircraft production was able to restart within 24 hours. Production was switched to various local alternative premises which included warehouses, garages and Shepperton film studios. A couple of days after the raid, barrage balloons were delivered and placed around the factories together with an increased number of anti-aircraft guns.

There is now a memorial to the '88', on site at Brooklands Museum, Weybridge, Surrey, listing the names of all those whose lives were lost. It was installed, along with an air raid shelter walk through experience, to commemorate the 80th anniversary of the raid in 2020. Little Billy's name is shown, in full, on the memorial. Some pictures showing the raid damage and the memorial are shown in the photos section of this book.

WIRELESS TELEGRAPHY ACTS, 1904–1926

LICENCE TO ESTABLISH WIRELESS TELEGRAPH STATION
FOR
EXPERIMENTS IN WIRELESS TELEGRAPHY

Mr. ..R.H. Shears and his son Roland George Shears as his agent........................

of ..52, Lytton Road, New Barnet, Herts..

hereinafter called "the Licensee" is hereby authorized to establish a wireless telegraph sending and receiving station for experimental purposes at the above address.

....

....

....

....

subject to the conditions overleaf and to the payment of a fee of   30/-   on the grant hereof (the receipt of which the Postmaster General hereby acknowledges) and a fee of   £1   on the anniversary of such date hereof in each year.

This licence is subject to withdrawal or modification at any time, either by specific notice in writing sent to the Licensee by post at the address shown above, or by means of a general notice in the *London Gazette* addressed to all holders of licences for experimental wireless telegraph transmitting stations.

Failure to send the call signal or to tune accurately to authorized frequencies, the use of unauthorized power or frequencies, or any other breach of the conditions or non-payment of fees will render it necessary for this licence to be cancelled. In event of cancellation no part of any fee paid in respect of the current year will be returned.

This licence replaces that dated the.12th December 1936, which with the call sign 2BXL which is hereby withdrawn, and should be returned to the address given below.
 Returned herewith

The Crystal Calibration Certificate is hereby withdrawn.

Issued on behalf of the } ..............P.K.Hammeans...............
Postmaster General   } ....6 February, 19.37..

All communications should be addressed to The Engineer-in-Chief, Radio Branch, General Post Office, London, E.C.1, quoting Reference W2./A.3089...............................

N.B.—Any change of address should be notified immediately.

E-in-C 429
(21825 36)

First G8KW licence, comfirmation February 1937

THE INCORPORATED RADIO SOCIETY OF GREAT BRITAIN

16 ASHRIDGE GARDENS,
LONDON, N.13

4th July, 1941

Dear O.M.,

I know you would wish to help our country in any way you can. Here is a way of doing so as a Radio Amateur.

The Navy, Army and Air Force are in need of the instruments mentioned at the foot of this letter for training purposes, and are appealing through me to Radio Amateurs to help.

Their need is urgent and immediate, and they will be pleased to receive apparatus as soon as possible, either as a gift or at the price you originally paid for it, provided that it is of good make and its performance is approximately equal to its original specification.

Do not regard the details given below as rigid ; for example, 0-100 ma. meters are wanted, but 0-50 ma. or 0-200 ma. would do. Only moving-coil type meters are wanted.

If you are a dealer and have instruments in stock, you can help the Services in this matter.

You should send all apparatus, carefully packed, by registered post to :—

> The Secretary,
> Wireless Telegraphy Board,
> C/o Admiralty,
> London, S.W.1.

You will hear direct from them. Don't forget to tie a label on the instrument itself with your name and address and mark it "GIFT" or "SALE".

If any of the instruments you are prepared to give or sell are in the hands of the G.P.O. please send particulars to The Secretary, Wireless Telegraphy Board, who will communicate with you in the event of any action regarding them being contemplated.

It is hoped that sufficient instruments will be forthcoming without resorting to those impounded with the G.P.O.

In making the request the authorities remarked that we have never failed them yet. This really means you as a Radio Amateur have never failed them, and I am sure you will not fail them now.

Thanking you, in anticipation, for your co-operation.

With best wishes,

Yours sincerely,

Alfred D. Gay,

President.

P.S. If you wish to ask any questions please write to The Secretary, Wireless Telegraphy Board, and not to me personally.

LIST OF APPARATUS REQUIRED BY THE NAVY, ARMY AND AIR FORCE

1. Avometer Model 7.
2. Avometer Model 40.
3. Avominor.
4. m.c. 0-10 milliam.
5. 0-50 milliam.
6. Thermal 0-1a.
7. Electrostatic 50-300 v.
8. Valve voltmeters 0-5/25/100 v.
9. Oscilloscopes.
10a. R.F. Oscillator.
11. Monitor C.R.T.

RSGB Appeal, July 1941, for Instruments for the Navy, Army and Air Force

COASTAL RADIO LIMITED

DIRECTORS
A. REDPATH
J. B. INGLIS
W. B. REDPATH

MARINE RADIO MANUFACTURERS

EDINBURGH, 7.

CONTRACTORS TO THE ADMIRALTY.

REGISTERED OFFICE
103 BRUNSWICK STREET
TELEPHONE 20795.

GEN/AR/CD
4387

22nd August 1941

R.J. Shears Esq.,
52, Lisson Road,
New Barnet,
HERTS.

Dear Sir,

ONE VALVE TZ05/20

      We have pleasure in enclosing our cheque in payment for your property as above which we received from the G.P.O. Radio Branch, and shall be glad if you will be good enough to sign and return the enclosed receipt.

      Thanking you.

                           Yours faithfully,
                           COASTAL RADIO LTD.,

                               Managing Director.

Compensation letter with payment for one Mullard TZ05/20 valve

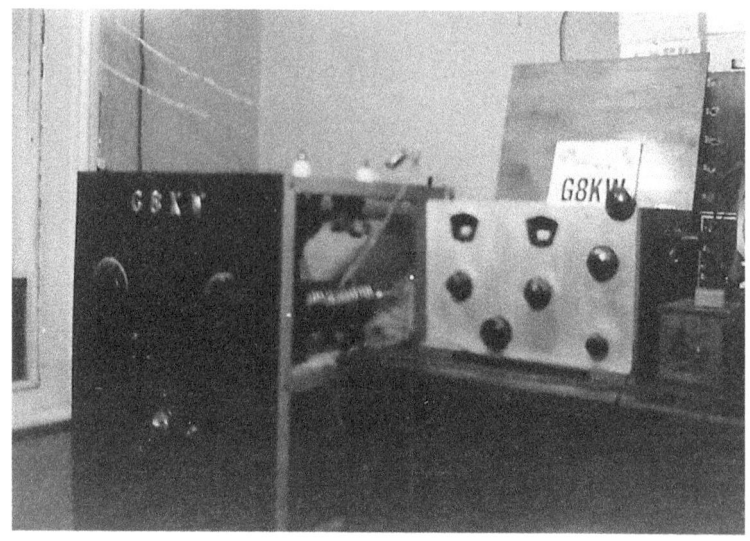

Rowley's early home G8KW radio station & radio amateur (QSL) postcard

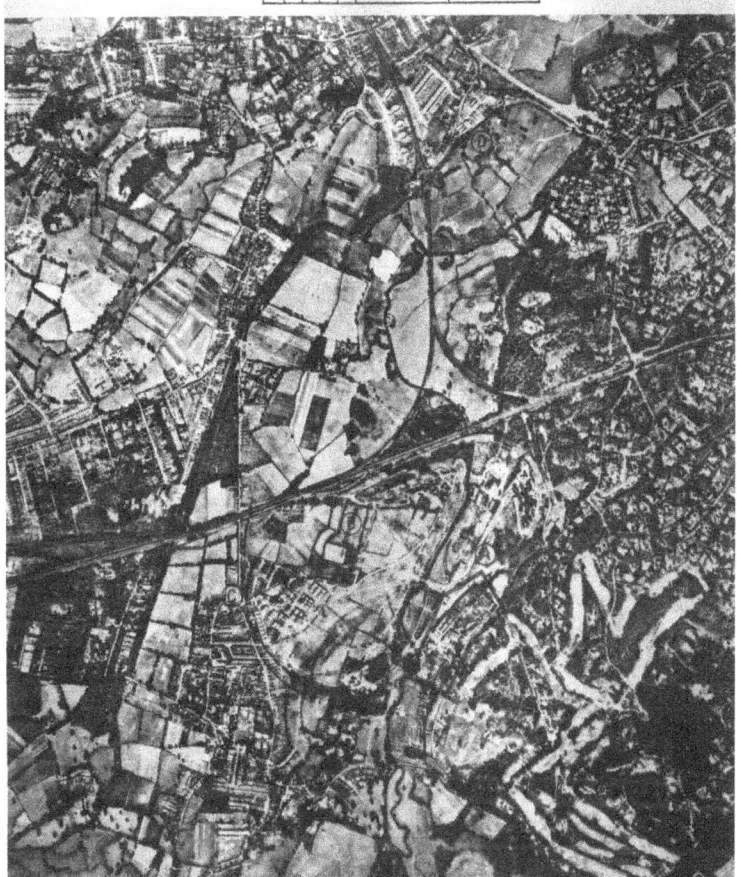

Vickers Aviation (Brooklands) Weybridge - Luftwaffe Target Map

Vickers Aviation (Brooklands) Weybridge - factory damage, 4th September 1940

Brooklands Museum memorial to the 88 killed on 4th September 1940

Chapter 7
Polygon Wireless Station (Abbassieh, Cairo)

A few weeks after the CSM incident, in October 1940, Rowley was given the opportunity to accompany a group of six Signals Officers on a visit to the Polygon Wireless Station (PWS), which was the General Headquarters (GHQ) main transmitting station and where the high-power transmitters were situated. Polygon, which was a transmitting station dating from the First World War, was located within the Abbassieh Garrison, on the outskirts of Cairo, about eight miles from GHQ in central Cairo, and three miles from Heliopolis aerodrome. Its position within the garrison was at the extreme end away from the garrison gates. Beyond the station was desert. In the early 1920s the station had been part of an Army wireless network which maintained communication with London and major centres for other countries within the British Empire – Calcutta, Hong Kong, Nairobi, Cape Town etc. Parts of the high masts used in those earlier times were lying horizontally on the ground when Rowley arrived and had been used to make pathways between the tents and the newer masts. Rowley was shown around the station by a knowledgeable corporal, Ken Ellis, who had recently been transferred to the Royal Signals from the Scots Guards, where he was a battalion signals sergeant, and turned out to be another radio ham with the call sign, G5KW. Sometime after meeting at Polygon, Ken was repatriated to the UK. He came back to Polygon later and was there as a major when Rowley left in early 1945. Their friendship continued after the war and later on they set up KW Electronics together.

This visit to Polygon would be a turning point in Rowley's Army career, as about a week later he was posted to Polygon as a member of No. 3 Company 3GHQ Signals MEF (Mediterranean Expeditionary Force), promoted to Corporal and elevated in trade rating to "Electrician Signals, Class 1". Formal recognition of this promotion was confirmed later, on 2nd April 1941. Rowley recalls that at Polygon there were seven No. 5 sets, each a 500 watt transmitter, installed in deep dugouts (underground shelters obscured from view) and two high-power No. 5 HP sets with 4 kilowatt transmitters. These sets were fixed, point to point, transmitters for long range communications developed in 1934 and manufactured by RTE and Plessey. Rowley described the No. 5 sets as single units standing at nearly 6 feet (1.7m) high and 3 feet (0.9m) wide and had a number of coloured knobs on the front panel which were "pushed in" or "pulled out" to change the frequency bands, not unlike a church organ. He further described the HP (high-power) versions as being in two cabinets, each of similar size to the No. 5 sets, but slightly taller at nearly 7 feet (2.1m) tall. One cabinet contained the power supply and the other contained the transmitter which he noted had four very large glass valves made by Mullard. In some installations there could be a third cabinet of similar size, containing an alternative frequency transmitter. The HP sets were used for high-speed telegraphy to the War Office in the UK and to Melbourne and Washington. The telegraphy tape transmitters were located in the GHQ Signal office in Cairo and connected to the transmitters at Polygon by a telephone cable line. The other transmitters (No. 5 sets) were used for hand Morse circuits to South Africa, Kenya, Khartoum, Baghdad, Calcutta and Singapore as well as the Western Desert.

At this time, the early north-African desert campaign, under Middle East Commander General Sir Archibald Wavell, was going well. The Italians (under Mussolini's command) had invaded Egypt from Libya in September 1940 but had been defeated by Wavell's army of around 50,000 men. Thousands of Italian soldiers had been captured and placed in prisoner of war camps, but Rowley notes they were allocated 30 or 40 Italian "prisoners of war" (POWs) to carry out various tasks on the station. One such task was digging the holes for the tents and erecting aerials, all under guard, of course, by one infantry man with a rifle. This was hardly necessary though as Rowley noted that "the Italians had lost the will to fight and spent much of their time singing, especially their favourite, O Sole Mio".

Rowley notes that Wavell had previously been advised not to extend his troops' advances further west than Tobruk because radio communications would be difficult as the Mobile Wireless Units did not have facilities to tune into high frequencies. Rowley's team at Polygon were therefore asked to look at improving the communications capability of the Heavy Wireless Units in order to improve radio communications from GHQ to the front around Tobruk, and beyond. Calculations showed that over such distances frequencies of around 10 megacycles would be necessary to give good daytime communications. The Heavy Wireless units only had No. 3 sets (manufactured around 1934 as a medium range transmitter/receiver) with the highest operating frequency of 5.5 megacycles. Rowley comments that no one at the Polygon Wireless Station had seen a No. 3 set before, when one arrived at Polygon installed on a very large truck. Along the sides of the vehicle were the lengths of steel tube to make up the 70-foot (21m) masts and on the roof was the mobile aerial. There was also a second vehicle which contained the power generator. An operator from the Heavy Wireless Section, who had accompanied the truck drivers, showed the Polygon team how to tune and test the transmitter and receiver. Using knowledge gained from his pre-war experiences of building transmitters and receivers, Rowley, along with others, worked day and night for seven days to modify the equipment. Working stage by stage, they managed to improve the frequency range of the receiver and achieved some success up to a top frequency of 9.8 MHz. They then applied the same technique to the transmitter and although the valves in this were not designed to work above 6 MHz, they were happy to achieve a 250 watt output at 9.8 MHz.

In order to give this first unit a good "air test" he got up one morning at about 3am and tuned the set to the 7.0 MHz amateur band. Using a fictitious Greek call sign he was able to communicate, and exchange reports, with several South American stations and he says he was able to return to bed feeling contented with the results. Rowley notes that at this time, the Germans had not advanced into Greece.

Once they had achieved success with the first unit, they were asked to improve six more mobile units in trucks. This was very time-consuming but not difficult as they had well documented the modifications done on the first one. After these were done, Rowley left Polygon for a three-week secondment to No. 3 Heavy Wireless Unit to test the effectiveness of the modifications and to be "on standby" in case of any problems with the sets during the advance. He joined the furthest advance Heavy Wireless Unit with their heavy trucks carrying the improved transmitters, aerials and generators at Marsa Matruh and went on, with that unit, through Sidi Barrani, Tobruk and on to Darnah (Derna). He comments that the equipment worked well and allowed all schedules to be maintained with GHQ. On his return trip Rowley called into Tobruk, to the Unit stationed there, to fix a replacement valve on a transmitter, then got a lift to Heliopolis Aerodrome courtesy of RAF Transport Command before making his way to Polygon Wireless Station.

After a very busy few months, in early 1941, Rowley was now back at Polygon and recounts being involved with more mundane activities for a while – erecting new aerials for new Allied positions across the desert. He notes that the Long Range Desert Group (LRDG) had penetrated further south across the western desert and had set up a small garrison at Kufra Oasis. Their only means of communication involved using a No. 19 set, run off a jeep battery, with a mobile 'whip' aerial. Consequently, a better aerial was needed at the 3GHQ receiving station, which was located about ten miles across the desert to the west of Cairo, near to an area known locally as 'the Dead City' due to the evidence of hundreds of old burials having taken place there. Now there were around 30-40 almost derelict cottages in the area. This location "was one of the best receiving sites" in the Cairo area as it was located in a small valley with sandstone hills on three sides which was useful in attenuating atmospheric noises to the radios. Rowley was issued with a (UK made) Matchless motorcycle for his trips across the desert to work on the communication improvements that were needed at the Dead City station and also to regularly inspect the equipment installed there. All of the high-speed telegraphy, receivers and aerials were contained in this small establishment.

Rowley notes that the terminating resistors, which had been made locally, were located in a large sand-proof wooden box, of about 6 cubic feet, with two large insulators sticking out of the top which were connected to the feeder line. The resistors, in their box, were sited around a mile from the Polygon transmitter.

Rowley recounts an amusing story which happened about a year later in 1942 when he was inspecting the resistors in the box. This occurred when one of the Radio Corporation of America (RCA) 7.5kW transmitters back at Polygon was being used for broadcasting music from the small studio they had built adjacent to the transmitter in the same dugout at Polygon. Rowley was carrying out test transmissions and he thought he should check the resistors to ensure they were not overheating. Arriving at the 'box' site on his Matchless he found around a dozen locals, with bare feet, dancing around the 'box' and laughing and clapping hands to the sound of the music. Rowley recalls he was astonished to hear the music and said to the locals, in his best Egyptian Arabic, that it was "Music from Allah"! To which one replied "ana mabsout owey" (I am very happy) and with that they walked off, laughing. After closing down the transmitter he inspected the resistors and found some corrosive material that had been causing the audio resonances.

On his return to Polygon after his desert trip with the No. 3 sets, Rowley recalls that he heard news that their Officer in Command (OC), Captain Hall, was to be posted to another unit and a week later at a farewell reception in the Sergeants' Mess, where he was now a member (although his sergeant's promotion was not formerly confirmed until later in November 1941), he learnt that their new captain had arrived in Egypt, and was a Canadian. A week or so after this, Captain Charles Kidd from the Royal Canadian Corps of Signals arrived at the station. His last post had been in the UK as OC in the War Office Signals Company at the UK end of the link with Polygon and Rowley noted that before the war, he had been a radio amateur in Nova Scotia. Rowley found Charles Kidd to be a likeable character and they had a good rapport, speaking the same language on technical subjects. He also remarked that Captain Kidd was not particularly regimental and gave the impression that he would probably cut 'red tape' to get the right result. Later during their work together this would prove to be correct!

Rowley recounts an interesting story about Captain Kidd who created quite a stir during his early days as Commanding Officer of No. 3 Company when he took delivery of new car. The car was a Chevrolet saloon with a V8 engine, in a green livery, and not the usual drab desert khaki, normally seen in the theatre of operations. Eventually an order came through to have it resprayed to the standard desert grey, to conform with regulations, so Captain Kidd found another way to personalise the car by adding some artwork to each of the two doors. Rowley commented that the artwork on both doors had patterns made up of radio circuit symbols, shaped like a scroll which gave the impression of a Royal crest. The design incorporated an electrical-based motto underneath it. Although there were mutterings from senior officers that these should be removed, they stayed, as no direct command to remove them was ever received.

Chapter 8

Panzer Tanks on the Russian Front and the Official Secrets Act

Those who knew Rowley might describe him as having a gregarious character with a good sense of humour who liked to talk and meet people. At this time in his life however, radio enthusiast Rowley chose to spend his spare time on his own, tuning around the wavelengths, sometimes on his own hand-built receivers.

Soon after Captain Kidd's arrival, Rowley was checking some communications receivers in his workshop. The receivers were used for monitoring transmissions and there was at least one receiver in each of the five 'dugouts' at Polygon. Most of the receivers were manufactured by USA companies (Hallicrafters, National Corporation, Hammarlund, RCA and Radio Manufacturing Engineers (RME)) as well as Stratton and Co Ltd of Birmingham, England, who made the 'Eddystone' range. These receivers were mostly used by people working away from their countries who wanted to listen to radio programmes from back home. Most of them tuned the frequencies from the medium wave band up to 30 megacycles (or the 10 metre band) but the Hammarlund Super-Pro tuned up higher to 40 megacycles. This bandwidth of 30-40 megacycles was of particular interest to Rowley as he had never heard a signal on this band other than the odd harmonic[1] from their own transmitter. He also knew that it was most suitable for 'line of sight communications'[2] and had not been internationally allocated to aero-nautical services.

---

[1] Harmonic frequency is another (often, unwanted) frequency generated at a multiple of the fundamental frequency.
[2] Line of sight communications, usually in a straight line from source to receiver without any major obstacles in between, e.g. mountains.

It was whilst testing this receiver with an aerial connected (rather than a test instrument) that he picked up voice transmissions spoken in German. He listened for about half an hour before calling his colleagues over to listen and to witness the event!

Rowley seemed to have a natural ability to pick up language skills (German, Arabic and, later, Greek) and by now he knew enough German to quickly guess that these on-air conversations were probably German tank commanders talking to each other and to their HQ, using simple microphones. He wondered where the signals were originating from, as the Germans were not yet in North Africa. Although a long way away, were they possibly from Eastern Europe or Russia? Rowley noted some place names that sounded Russian so, with the help of colleagues, put together a basic directional aerial, which could be rotated, to allow a fairly accurate compass bearing to be established.

All the officers had been attending a meeting at GHQ, but as soon as Captain Kidd returned to the station Rowley reported his findings and suggested that he needed a cross-reference bearing from another location (possibly, Palestine) to establish the exact location. Captain Kidd reported Rowley's discovery to GHQ immediately and told him to expect a visit tomorrow morning from senior officers, whom Rowley recalls were often referred to as "The Brass Hats". The following morning a staff car arrived and Rowley was visited in his workshop by a staff brigadier, a colonel, and a major, all from Military Intelligence, together with another major from the Signals.

Fortunately, the propagation conditions were good and Rowley was able to demonstrate a repeat of what he had heard on the first day. The Signals Major commented that he had no knowledge of this frequency being used for anything other than "line of sight communications" so it appeared that the Germans had not realised that signals for this type of communication could, under certain atmospheric conditions, be heard hundreds or thousands of kilometres away.

The officers asked Rowley to make a second directional aerial, which he did, and this was flown by the RAF, on the same day, from Heliopolis to Palestine where there was an Intercept Wireless Station. After the aerial was installed and connected in Palestine, Rowley was able to get an accurate cross reference between the two sites and confirm that the German Panzer tanks were positioned along the Polish/Russian Front. This was well in advance of Hitler's invasion of Russia, Operation Barbarossa[1], which would commence on 22nd June 1941. The Intelligence officers were delighted about this news and a continual monitoring and intelligence gathering programme was put in place.

A few days later two majors, who were from SIME (Security Intelligence Middle East), visited again and asked Captain Kidd if they could speak to Rowley in private. The officers questioned him about his background and, recognising his expertise in Morse and signals work, asked him to sign the Official Secrets Act as they wanted to impart some highly secret information to him. They informed him that their job involved rounding up and interrogating suspect spies in Cairo, some of whom were passing messages by wireless to the enemy. They had a project that was about to be implemented and asked him if he would be interested in joining SIME to work on it. Rowley responded with a "yes". They explained that their Brigadier would contact Rowley's Brigadier (Eric Coles, G2EC) to make arrangements for his secondment to SIME for the project. He would still be able to carry out his signals work when not working on the special project. Rowley questioned whether Captain Kidd would be told about this project. The officers informed Rowley that Captain Kidd would only be told that he was to be involved in a Top Secret intelligence gathering project and that he was not to disclose details of the project to any of the staff at Polygon, nor to any other person, not even his family back in the UK.

When the officers had left, Rowley comments that it left him "feeling somewhat intrigued and bewildered".

---

[1] Operation Barbarossa was the invasion of the Soviet Union by Nazi Germany and its Axis allies.

Chapter 9
The Deception Game Begins

A few days after the visit from the intelligence officers, Rowley was collected by one of the majors and taken to GHQ Middle East command in Cairo (known as Grey Pillars or, locally, as The Secret Building). He met with a colonel, a captain and the two majors (whom he had previously met) where the role and responsibilities of SIME were explained to him.

SIME was based in Cairo, having been created in December 1939, and was under the control of Brigadier Raymond Maunsell. It was effectively the local arm of MI5 and had links to all the other security services as well as the 'double cross' XX Committee, (a double cross, counter-espionage unit comprising representatives of the military service intelligence agencies) which assessed intelligence from the large number of turned agents and provided disinformation aimed at deceiving their German controllers.

The colonel advised that SIME was responsible for all aspects of security in the Middle East, sought intelligence information and worked closely with the Military Police and other bodies. His section of SIME traced foreign agents arriving in the Middle East area as well as agents who had been resident for longer periods and had infiltrated the armed forces and services because they had sympathies towards the enemy. He explained that they currently had a German agent in custody at one of their safe houses. He'd been picked up in Cairo two weeks ago, whilst looking for accommodation, and brought in for questioning. The agent had admitted arriving in a dinghy, having left a U-boat offshore, and landed on a deserted beach on the Nile Delta, near Alexandria. In the house, which he had planned to lease, they had found a false passport and identity papers, half a dozen reading books, clothing and a number of gold coins (mostly sovereigns).

This individual, named as 'Alex' by the officers, had been interrogated every day since being brought in and had agreed to co-operate. Rowley was told that Alex, who was in his early thirties, had been born in Armenia and then taken to Berlin as a young boy, where his father was a diplomat. He had obtained an engineering degree at Berlin University and was able to speak fluent Berliner Deutsch (dialect of Berlin and surrounding areas) as well as good English. He held an amateur radio licence, issued in Germany by the Deutscher Amateur Sender Dienst (DASD). In order to obtain a transmitting licence and join the DASD, Alex would have needed to be a good member of the Nazi party as well as being able to meet the international Morse standard (12 words per minute) and to pass a technical exam. Alex considered himself to be a good Morse operator and this is why he had been recruited to attend a spy school where he had been taught coded message procedures and how to change the 'key' for every message sent or received.

The Intelligence Section colonel told Rowley that Alex had already revealed the systems for encoding and decoding plus all the allocated frequencies. After much questioning, Alex had insisted that no special code or sign had been devised to inform his German masters that he had been caught. Rowley notes, later in his memoirs, that the interrogation of Alex was done by a brilliant linguist and tough interrogator called 'Major Max', although Rowley says he never knew his full name!

Alex had told them that, in 1941, Germany did not have access to a small transmitter/receiver that would fit into a suitcase that he could have brought with him. He had been told that he could buy an American communications receiver, possibly a Hallicrafters model, (Sky Champion) from a shop in Cairo – presumably by using the gold he had with him. Alex was also expected to build a transmitter after buying the parts from shops in Cairo.

Rowley was told that he should now take on the life of Alex and act as though he was serving the 'Vaterland'[1] – figuratively speaking of course!

Rowley confirmed that he could build a transmitter, and that would take about two weeks once he had the necessary equipment. By chance there had been a recent delivery to Polygon Wireless Station of transmitter and receiver equipment that had been shipped from Addis Ababa, captured after Mussolini's invasion and war in Abyssinia of 1938. Some of these parts would be usable.

He had a number of questions about Alex's Morse style, the communication frequencies and schedules and the location of the contact station, but probably the most important question was whether any recordings had been made by the Germans of Alex's style in sending Morse and whether the operator back in Germany could recognise his style. The sending of Morse is like handwriting and varies from person to person. Each sender has their own recognisable operating characteristics (known as their 'fist') which comes from the rhythm and time pacing between the words and letters (dots, dashes and pauses). If Alex's fist was recognisable, Rowley needed to spend time with him so that he could emulate his style.

Rowley was instructed to discreetly start the construction of the transmitter. Before he left the meeting, he was asked what it would cost to buy the Sky Champion receiver. Guessing that he would need 10,000-15,000 Egyptian Piastres (at the time, this equated to approximately £150), he was told that this money would be made available to him and that he should purchase the Sky Champion receiver from the shop that Alex had been advised to go to.

A few days after the meeting, Rowley received the 15,000 Piastres, in bank notes, accompanied by a Military-issued 'Green Pass', bearing his photograph (taken whilst at Grey Pillars), which

---

[1] Vaterland – German, literally meaning Fatherland, a nationalistic term used to unite Nazi Germany in the ways of ancient Germany.

authorised him to 'be in any place, at any time and in any dress'. In a note from SIME, which came with the package, Rowley was advised to wear civilian clothes to do his "receiver shopping" in Sharia Emad-el-Dine, Cairo. After seeking advice from an experienced corporal, who had served in WWI, on where to buy a suit, he used 350 Piastres to buy a second-hand one from a shop within the Abbassieh Garrison then headed out, via the Heliopolis tram, to buy the receiver and a pair of headphones. Rowley notes that the particular receiver he purchased did have an inbuilt loudspeaker but this would be disconnected once the headphones were plugged in. On returning to Polygon, he hid the package in the stores. The importance of 'Secrecy and Security' were now very apparent to Rowley.

Chapter 10
Preparing to Contact the Enemy

Rowley now needed access to a private workshop area at Polygon where he could construct the transmitter and test this as well as the receiver. He had identified a small building of about 15ft by 12ft in the middle of the compound, which had originally been built to house an aerial tuning unit for the old long-wave transmitter. Captain Kidd agreed that the current contents of the building could be stored elsewhere, arranged for a bench to be constructed to allow Rowley to work there and also provided a desk and chairs. Rowley changed the lock and kept the keys and Captain Kidd later arranged for a sign to be made and affixed to the outside of the door which read "Admission to this workshop only to authorised personnel".

Whilst Rowley made a start on testing the new receiver and began to gather all the components and materials needed to construct the transmitter, the interrogation of Alex had yielded more information. He had revealed that one of the six books in his possession, and always carried with him, was his 'key' to both enciphering and deciphering of the messages. This was the novel *Gone with the Wind* (American edition).

Amongst Alex's possessions were six graph pads where each page was printed with 5mm squares for use as a matrix. He explained that he had been taught to encipher messages, for security, from the plain English text using a double transposition method using the matrix and the 'key' book to find the text to be transmitted, which would be in five letter groups. Rowley notes that this system was common for Military or Government messages which needed to be encrypted for security reasons. As determined by his German masters in Berlin, there were additional security measures applied to the encryption system. Message 1 would start on a particular page, line and specific word, message 2 would start on a different page and details of this would have been given at the end of message 1. Alex still maintained that his 'fist' had not been recorded and that he would not be sending messages to any operators he had trained with.

The intelligence officers started working on the contents of the first messages that Rowley would be expected to send and soon he had his first meeting with Alex at a SIME safe house. He had taken some Morse code training equipment, including two pairs of headphones and two Morse keys, with him. He recalls being led into a sparsely furnished room where he saw Alex talking with a SIME officer. The conversation immediately stopped when he entered and Rowley comments that it did not sound like part of an interrogation. He was not formally introduced to Alex. One of his colleagues simply said, "Sergeant here has brought along a Morse Oscillator and would like to have a 'QSO' (radio conversation) with you." Rowley set up his equipment and passed a pair of headphones and a Morse key to Alex, who adjusted both to his liking. Rowley then tapped out an internationally recognisable 'Q' code 'QRV' (are you ready?) to which Alex replied 'QRV' (I am ready). Rowley sent him plain language and five-letter group messages for about five minutes and at 18-20 words per minute. Alex copied these and sent them back with ease. Rowley found his style easy to copy but recognised it was a little different to his own style. These differences, such as "slightly clipped dots" could probably be corrected by adjustment to the Morse key. Alex seemed to be quite relaxed during the session but also looked relieved when it was over. In appearance, Alex reminded Rowley of a "Turkish gentleman" he had met a few years earlier. He was probably "in his early thirties", of medium build with an athletic appearance. He had a bushy moustache over his top lip but was otherwise clean shaven. He was not readily identifiable as an indigenous German which was probably why his German masters chose him for service in Egypt.

Rowley returned to Polygon to continue his work on designing the transmitter, power supply and aerial. He notes that he was fortunate to have the help of a lance corporal instrument mechanic, called Scottie, with this task, who could continue to assemble the equipment, based on Rowley's design, whilst Rowley was away from the base at Grey Pillars or elsewhere. During the next week, they both worked ten to twelve hours each day and secretly completed the assembly work, then switched it on to test it.

Rowley hadn't expected everything to function so well for the first test, as many of the components had been lying around for four years in difficult climatic conditions and a lack of suitable test equipment had prevented individual component testing prior to assembly. After a couple of weeks of 'bug' testing and carrying out the appropriate air tests with both Baghdad and Khartoum stations for frequency and stability, Rowley felt confident the equipment was ready for use on 'Operation Cheese', this being the code name given by SIME for the project he was now involved with. Later in his memoirs, Rowley documents that he met with Alex on two occasions and was later told that Alex was put in jail in Cairo.

Chapter 11
Assuming a New Identity for Operation Cheese

Rowley phoned his colleagues at SIME with the good news that the equipment was ready for use, and they agreed to visit him the next day to discuss establishing radio contact with the German military intelligence known as the Abwehr.

Two SIME officers (a major and a captain) visited Rowley in his workshop at the Polygon station with a large wad of papers. Pointing to the papers, the officers explained the call procedures that Alex had revealed to them.

Alex had advised that he was to make contact on a specific frequency with a given call sign at precisely 16.00 hours GMT for two minutes. If there was no contact, he was to try again after one hour and again after two hours. If still no contact after this time he was to try again the following day at 16.00 hours GMT but on a different frequency and with a different call sign. He said this was to be the procedure for seven days and the next week he would revert back to the same procedure as the previous week, until contact was made.

They all agreed to try to establish contact that same evening and Rowley was handed the wad of papers which had details of the frequencies and call signs. He had procured a strong safe in which to store this information and had positioned it below the floor in the workshop.

The officers advised that, during questioning, Alex had revealed that the German Intelligence (Abwehr) receiving location was likely to be Sofia in Bulgaria, but this was expected to change. With this information in mind Rowley knew that he had to modify the aerial mast so that the aerial could be moved by around 40 degrees to allow a stronger signal into Sofia.

Rowley was told that the 'Y' sections (British Army Signals Intelligence sites) in Cyprus and Palestine would be monitoring the frequencies to assist with direction finding, if and when the Germans replied. SIME had prepared the first encoded message for Rowley to send which was along the lines of "WE ARE PLEASED TO ESTABLISH CONTACT AT LAST AND WAS THERE A MESSAGE FOR ME?"

The officers left and Rowley returned to his workshop in time for a chat before the first schedule time. At precisely 16.00 hours Rowley commenced his message in Morse but there was no reply from the Germans. He tried again one hour later, but again there was no reply. Rowley noticed the disappointment on the faces of his two visitors and advised them that the receiving stations were probably checking the transmissions to make sure that the signals were originating from the Cairo area, before they sent a reply.

The same officers arrived again the next evening and Rowley started his messaging at the set time. This time there was a reply and Rowley notes that "the three of us cheered and shook hands". The Morse message read "GE VY PSED TO QSO U – UR SIGS RST 569 ERE QTC1 QRV" Using International abbreviations, this translated as "GOOD EVENING – VERY PLEASED TO CONTACT YOU. YOUR SIGNALS ARE READABILITY 5, STRENGTH 6, TONE 9. HERE I HAVE ONE MESSAGE, ARE YOU READY?" Rowley replied "R QRV K" (OK I am ready) and the operator started to send an enciphered message in five letter groups which took eight minutes to come through. Rowley acknowledged receipt and asked them to wait 30 minutes. The message, which took nearly 30 minutes to decipher, was enquiring whether any useful intelligence had been gathered and requested that he should send a full report tomorrow.

Rowley sent the prepared, and already enciphered, response which read:

"I AM LIVING NEAR TO MIDDLE EAST HEADQUARTERS. FOR SECURITY REASONS MUST MAKE SHORT TRANSMISSIONS. THERE IS MUCH GENERAL INTELLIGENCE AVAILABLE HERE. SUGGEST YOU SUPPLY ME WITH A PRIORITY LIST FOR INTELLIGENCE GATHERING. I WILL SEEK THE INFORMATION WHICH YOU REQUIRE AS PRIORITY." After agreeing to meet the next day, at the same frequency but half an hour later, Rowley signed off and closed down the station.

Contact next day went according to schedule and the Abwehr response read: "YOUR SUGGESTION APPROVED – WE WILL HAVE MESSAGE WITH DETAILS TOMORROW – SAME TIME AS TODAY BUT CHANGE FREQUENCY AND CALL SIGN". Rowley acknowledged the message and sent GN (goodnight).

Rowley's Intelligence colleagues were very keen to know what the German Intelligence (Abwehr) wished to know. Everyone involved realised that the next stage of exchanging messages would have to include some correct information to encourage confidence to be built up. It was well known to SIME that there were several spies from Germany and its major allies in Egypt who had not yet been apprehended and that made it possible for German Intelligence to cross check any information which they received from their agent (Rowley).

The next series of messages from the Abwehr were requests for information about troop movements, numbers of artillery weapons, numbers and types of tanks, personnel carriers etc. The Germans were probably aware of ships from the UK, Australia, New Zealand, South Africa and India arriving in the Suez Canal area and that troops and equipment needed to be conveyed either by road or rail to the Western Desert. Either way the routing had to be via Cairo or close to the metropolis.

Much of the information required to answer those requests was obtained by SIME from 'G Ops' (General Operations) and other military sources in Cairo. It was sometimes necessary to seek the sanction of the new Commander-in-Chief of Middle East Command, Sir Claude Auchinleck, due to the sensitivity of the requests.

So began Rowley's work on the Cheese project, a communication channel responsible for feeding a great deal of misinformation about Allied war plans and troop movements back to the German military intelligence (Abwehr) radio receiving stations in Europe between 1941 and 1944. SIME masterminded the sending of false information alongside a selection of true information which they could give away without compromising the safety of troops or success of military operations. SIME were aware of the opportunities of sending false information back to the Abwehr and then on to the German desert commanders but knew that sending too much false information would have resulted in the termination of the Cheese project. A balanced mix of accurate as well as false information provided to the Abwehr allowed the team to successfully operate the Cheese project until well after the battles of El Alamein and the defeat of the German Army in North Africa.

Rowley notes that, over the next few months in 1941, he sent and received dozens of messages with contact being made with the Abwehr three or four times a week. It appeared that each side was testing the other. Most of the questions Rowley received were about the desert campaign, and answers were provided "without giving away any monumental military intelligence".

At some stage the fictitious name of imaginary agent 'Paul Nicosoff' had been invented by the SIME intelligence team, apparently based on a play of the words 'pull knickers off' which would have been considered schoolboy humour at the time. Although Rowley made frequent mentions of Cheese in his memoirs he never included the name of Nicosoff in any of his notes.

Rowley noted that Churchill was informed about the Cheese project and had expressed "his interest and satisfaction" with it. Rowley later missed the opportunity to meet Churchill when he visited Military Intelligence in Cairo as he had a tight schedule and Rowley was busy handling Abwehr traffic at the time.

Rowley's promotion to lance sergeant was formerly confirmed on the 19th November 1941. His promotion to full sergeant was confirmed on the 27th May 1942 but Rowley noted that this happened "in the field" within a few weeks of the first promotion.

Chapter 12
A Padded Cell and the Hunt for an Understudy!

Sometime in early 1942, after nearly two years in desert conditions and regularly working twelve-hour days to ensure the success of the Cheese project, Rowley succumbed to sand-fly fever and a septic throat, coupled with a temperature of 103 degrees F (39.5 degrees C). The Garrison Medical Officer insisted that he be hospitalised which "caused a bit of a flurry around the SIME office". It unfortunately happened at a time when extremely sensitive messaging with the Abwehr regarding military action in the desert was taking place and Rowley needed to be available for sending the messages at pre-arranged times. As SIME did not wish Rowley to be seen being wheeled in and out of hospital wards, he was admitted to a remote area of the 5th South African hospital – chosen because of its close proximity to Abbassieh Garrison (Polygon WS). For reasons of secrecy, he wasn't formally admitted, but was put into a "padded cell", normally reserved for cases of violent drunkenness. He was then watched over by a South African medical team for nearly two weeks. Because of the need to continue regular contact with the Abwehr, Rowley was taken to and from the Abbassieh Garrison by ambulance to meet the transmission timelines. At the Abbassieh entrance the ambulance was always met by Major James Robertson, whom Rowley was now working with. The two South African nurses told Rowley how scared they had first felt when ordered to pick up a British sergeant from the padded cell at the hospital!

Once the critical messages had been sent in the required timeline, Rowley sent another message to say he was going to the

'Canal Zone' to gather some intelligence and would call again in four days. It was hoped this would buy him some time in which to fully recover. Rowley's dedication to duty on this occasion was later recognised by his senior officers in his commendation for a British Empire Medal.

This illness episode made the Intelligence Officers at SIME realise that they should have contingency plans in place so that if anything serious should happen to Rowley, the operation of the Cheese channel could continue. After Rowley had recovered, there was a lengthy discussion at Grey Pillars about the possibility of introducing a back-up operator without the Abwehr realising. Rowley believed it was risky to take on another Signals operator as they might not be able to emulate his fist, which would then be noticed by the Abwehr. Rowley requested that the person chosen to be his back-up should have no previous knowledge of Morse so that he could train them from scratch in his style. This was agreed and Major Robertson took it upon himself to make enquiries to find somebody who "fitted the bill". He told Rowley that he expected this task of finding the right person and bringing them from the UK would take around five to six weeks. He also told Rowley to try to stay out of hospital for the duration of the war!

Chapter 13

More Portions of Cheese and a Commission

With his health restored Rowley returned to his regular tasks of encoding, decoding, receiving and sending messages. Before his illness, he had started to record the different styles of the German Abwehr operatives transmitting to him as he had noticed that several changes of operators had been made recently. He gave each a reference number and a fictitious name in case the pattern of operator changes proved useful to British Intelligence in the future.

Rowley had noticed that on messages that he was receiving from the Germans sometimes an additional operator came on air again after the initial signoff (NW QRU – now I have nothing further for you) and would then send an extra message in a different "chattier" style. Rowley gave this operator the name of 'Wolfgang' and thought that he had probably been a radio amateur pre-war, because he used known international abbreviations during his messages, and was now a signals superintendent or officer in charge at the Abwehr radio station. Once decoded, 'Wolfgang's' message read "GE OM TNX QRK 73 ES SLEEP WELL" which was "GOOD EVENING OLD MAN", a friendly and common greeting for radio amateurs to use, "THANKS FOR THE SIGNAL REPORT KIND REGARDS AND SLEEP WELL". These "chattier" messages were similar in tone each time and generally came once a week, but one month after they started Rowley noted a one-off variation to the message from 'Wolfgang' which included an additional special greeting "WISH U WELL". Rowley started keeping notes to record when such special additional messages arrived. He wondered whether 'Wolfgang' was trying to discreetly tell him something. He cross-referenced the special message dates with his diary and found their significance. They were all received on dates when Luftwaffe night air raids over Cairo, the Suez towns and Alexandria had taken place. It appeared that Wolfgang was trying to tell Rowley something. Whenever the 'special message' was received, over the next six months, SIME alerted the RAF and the anti-aircraft artillery about the expected air raids. Rowley notes that after that time the Luftwaffe concentrated more on the ground movements of military personnel in the desert campaign. His location was only about a kilometre from the Heliopolis airfield boundary but only a few bombs hit that area. Most bombs landed in the desert and, on one occasion, three out of twelve Luftwaffe planes taking part in a raid were destroyed by an RAF squadron who caught them as they returned northwards over the Mediterranean.

In early 1942, Rowley sent a message to the Abwehr advising them he would be away from the base for five days to collect intelligence information and arranged a time and date for their next call. The reason for this temporary lack of activity was that he was due to attend a War Office Selection Board (WOSB)[1].

During 1941, Rowley had been recommended for a commission and orders had come through from the War Office in London for him to be repatriated to the UK to attend a six-month OCTU (Officers Cadet Training Unit) course. However, because Captain Kidd wanted to keep him on at Polygon as a Technical Officer and SIME wished to keep him on the Cheese Project, it had been agreed that they would seek alternative arrangements for Rowley to be promoted.

Rowley had already attended an interview at Grey Pillars where he was interviewed by a panel of six officers (none below the rank of colonel) and chaired by Brigadier Eric Cole, Royal Signals, who later became Major-General. Following the session of questions, he

---

[1] WOSB (War Office Selection Board) was a scheme devised by psychiatrists during the Second World War to select potential officers for the British Army. It was based on psychological methods and was later used by many organisations in their recruitment process.

was informed he would be attending a WOSB at Maadi, on the outskirts of Cairo. It was explained that attendance at this was a pre-requisite to attending an OCTU course but that in certain exemplary circumstances, the need for attending that course could be waived.

At the WOSB, with around 30 other candidates from various British Army Regiments and Corps, Rowley was put through a five-day intensive exercise to test his leadership skills, his initiative, responsibility and technical knowledge. At the end of the five days, he was informed that he had been successful and had exceeded the required standard. On this occasion half of the candidates passed.

A few days after his return to Polygon, "GHQ Unit Orders" were published and appeared on the GHQ Signals notice board to announce that Sgt R G Shears was commissioned with the rank of 2nd Lieutenant on 24th March 1942. His General List Commission, as a 2nd Lieutenant within SIME, was formalised much later on the 22nd July 1943 and was classified as an 'in the field' appointment. This arrangement was only available to members of MI5 (SIME), MI6 ('A' Force/SIS) or SOE during times of war. Once commissioned within SIME, he was effectively on loan to the GHQ Signals and this arrangement continued until October 1944.

In Rowley's case, the need for a formal OCTU course had been waived but, at the end of the war, its absence would lead to a number of bureaucratic challenges from the Royal Signals and the War Office in London, before his next posting to Germany could be agreed.

Rowley notes that, as a result of his commission, he was then able to frequent the Officers' Mess instead of the Sergeants' Mess. This was a building of colonial design, probably from the 1920s, just beyond the periphery of Polygon but still within the Abbassieh Garrison. It had a small garden, a splendid dining room, a well-equipped kitchen and staff accommodation for up to ten officers. Rowley knew all the officers there, the most senior being Charles Kidd (Royal Canadian Corps of Signals), who was now a major. Apart from himself and Major Kidd, there were four other officers from the Royal Signals, three from Rhodesian Signals and one from the South African Signals.

Rowley describes purchasing his new tropical khaki uniform, with two single 'pips', one for each epaulet. The officer-style peaked cap he required had proved something of a procurement problem, so he had managed to acquire a cap from his friends in the 5th South African Signals. The design of this was not so rigid in style as the British officers' cap as it was made of a soft felt and was not unlike that worn by the Americans. This soft-styled cap proved very useful later when he was in Greece in 1944.

Rowley's promotion (in the field) to full lieutenant happened within three months of being promoted to 2nd Lieutenant. He learned about this when told to see Brigadier Maunsell in advance of a meeting at Grey Pillars. He arrived wearing his newly purchased uniform and was promptly reprimanded for being improperly dressed. Confused by this, he was then told that he should be wearing two sets of pips, rather than one, as his promotion to full lieutenant had appeared in yesterday's GHQ orders. The Brigadier congratulated him and Rowley went off to join the meeting with his SIME colleagues. The announcement for his promotion to lieutenant appeared in the London Gazette on 10th March 1944.

Chapter 14
We Need More Funds…

Around the time of his promotion, the Abwehr were asking for specific information about Allied advances in the desert. Although SIME had the information, sending it might compromise some of the troops fighting there. Rowley was therefore asked to send only part of a message to the Abwehr before faking a transmitter failure which would prevent the rest of the crucial information from being sent. Rowley put an intermittent condition on the transmitter for about four to five minutes which then led to a complete failure at a suitable point in the message sending. He completed the rest of the message about 48 hours later and announced that "he had temporarily repaired the transmitter". The time between the messages allowed the impending initial military action to be completed in the desert. It was hoped that the accuracy of the information sent would enhance the reputation and reliability of Cheese in the eyes of the Abwehr and provide the SIME team with an opportunity to request more funds.

At a meeting with his SIME colleagues the next day they agreed the content of their next message. It seemed plausible that an 'undercover agent' living in Cairo would, by now, be running low on cash after paying his rent and many other expenses. It was decided to send a message requesting funds and using the transmitter failure story to strengthen this need for cash. The next evening, Rowley sent an encoded message which read:

"MY TRANSMITTER URGENTLY REQUIRES ATTENTION. TUBES (VALVES) AND SEVERAL COMPONENTS MUST BE REPLACED TO PREVENT FURTHER MALFUNCTION. FUNDS DESPERATELY LOW DUE TO HEAVY EXPENSES FOR RENT,

LIVING COSTS AND INFORMATION GATHERING. ADVISE ON NEXT SCHEDULED TIME."

Five days later a reply from the Germans was received and decoded:

"WE UNDERSTAND YOUR POSITION. FUNDS WILL BE CARRIED BY COURIER. EXPECT DELIVERY TO LOCAL HOUSE KNOWN TO YOU IN 10 TO 14 DAYS."

Rowley was surprised at the use of a courier, but some of his Intelligence colleagues who had worked in the diplomatic service in Turkey, assured him that this was usual practice. The funds would probably travel to Istanbul, then Beirut, Haifa, Tel Aviv and Kantara – the crossing point into Egypt – and then finally to "the local safe house" in Heliopolis, a suburb of Cairo. At each stage of the journey the package would be signed for.

Rowley was advised of the arrival of the funds after four extremely well-armed SIME agents and Military Police delivered it to an office in Grey Pillars after collecting it from the safe house. Rowley notes that the package was "surprisingly heavy" and he was there to witness its opening. The funds consisted entirely of gold coins, mostly Sovereigns (Victoria, George and Edward versions) but also French and Dutch plus about 20 coins from the USA. They set about "valuing the haul" and a quick call to Barclays Bank (Home & Colonial) in Cairo (Rowley's bank) to ascertain the value revealed the total was over £15,000 which in today's money (2025) would be around £900,000. Rowley comments that the consignment of coins was promptly paid into the British Government Exchequer account.

Whilst awaiting the funds, the Abwehr had been fed the story that temporary repairs to the transmitter continued and that he was only able to operate at much reduced power until he could obtain replacement valves and components.

Polygon Wireless Station had just received a large consignment from the UK of No. 5 sets with power supply units as well as spare parts and replacement valves. Rowley obtained permission to use some of these spares which also included a linear amplifier and a larger power supply to improve the performance of his existing transmitter. Although the original transmitter still worked well, the addition of the linear amplifier would double the power output to the aerial. This would help when there was interference from other stations on the same frequency or atmospheric conditions were bad. The Abwehr, on a subsequent 'chatty' message exchange, even complimented Rowley on the good signal quality and strength. Rowley notes that they "most probably thought that their money had been well spent".

Chapter 15
A Trainee for the Cheese Team

Deception transmissions were continuing as part of the normal routine for some time after the arrival of the funding. Then Rowley received a telephone call from Major Robertson to say that Intelligence had found him a suitable pupil to train as his 'back-up' and they would be arriving by staff car tomorrow morning.

Rowley had already acquired a Morse code practice set with two Morse keys and two pairs of headphones. He met his trainee as she stepped out of a staff car on arrival at Polygon. He was surprised to see that his trainee was a young, blonde, attractive Junior Commander from the Auxiliary Territorial Service (ATS). Her name was Anne, and she was probably in her late twenties. Anne was one of the few women who had volunteered for overseas service. She had previously been supervising numerous telephone exchanges for 'Telecommunications Middle East' (TME) until about fifteen months ago when she was repatriated to the UK to have a baby. She had applied for a new posting and, with the help of a brigadier uncle in the War Office, she had got back to the Middle East whilst her mother took charge of the baby. James Robertson had told her about the secret nature of the work she would be doing and she was enthusiastic about her new role and remarked that hard work did not worry her. As requested, she had no knowledge of Morse or the enciphering of messages. She could play the piano quite well which Rowley told her would enable her to learn Morse quite easily as "Morse is similar to a musical sound". He explained the basics of Morse code to her and the need for her to learn to emulate his fist over time. This would mean that she could take over from him, when he was needed on other operations, and the Abwehr would not be alerted to a different operator. Anne had been told to report to Rowley five days a week, at 10am each day, for up to two hours practising Morse Code and, in the afternoons, she would be at the SIME offices to learn about code enciphering and deciphering. Rowley wondered whether any of his colleagues had seen Anne arriving and what he would say to them about the work she was about to start. Rowley confirmed to James Robertson that she was a good candidate and estimated it would take around two to three months to train her.

Chapter 16
Improving Desert Communications at Polygon Wireless Station

At the time that Anne arrived, Rowley notes that he was working on SIME intelligence matters most evenings whilst carrying out his Signals job during the day, which involved installation and maintenance of transmitters and receivers as well as upgrades and improvement to the communications set up at Polygon.

New and more powerful equipment was being delivered from both the USA and UK as part of the build-up of Allied resources in North Africa before the final push at El Alamein (summer 1942) and Operation Torch (November 1942). Just after Anne arrived, Rowley describes being called to Major Charles Kidd's office where he was asked to supervise the installation of a new powerful 15 kilowatt transmitter plus an extra 7.5 kilowatt one which had just been delivered to Polygon. London wanted them installed as soon as possible for use on the high-speed telegraphy circuit to the War Office. This would release their existing 7.5kW transmitter for use on other circuits. Rowley's team took two and a half days to unpack the new transmitters, which had been delivered by ship to Alexandria as part of a larger consignment of transmitters which were due to be installed elsewhere. Rowley noted that the delivery instructions for the consignment read " 2 X 7.5 kW transmitters to RAF (Middle East), 2 X 7.5 kW transmitters to MI6 (Middle East), 1 x 15 kW & 1 x 7.5 kW transmitter to 3 GHQ Signals (Polygon)".

Work was already underway for the installation of the new transmitters in the south dug out where it would be adjacent to the existing 7.5 kW transmitter, which Rowley notes had functioned well on the War Office high speed telegraphy link over the last six months.

By the end of the fourth week both transmitters had been fully installed and tested and were ready for duty. These two latest additions gave them a total of 16 x No. 5 sets and 4 x No. 5 HP (high power) sets made by Plessey (UK) plus 3 x Radio Corporation of America (RCA) sets from USA. All the transmitters were connected by underground cables which terminated in the GHQ Signals Office in the Grey Pillars building in Cairo. This was where all the signals Morse operators sent and received messages from London, Karachi, Khartoum, New Delhi, Washington, Hong Kong, Melbourne, Baghdad, Basra, Damascus and Tripoli, along with several local circuits to the Desert Army HQ, Corps HQ, Long Range Desert Group (LRDG), Kufrah Oasis, and Palestine groups.

The Signals staff at Polygon, who were mostly Instrument Mechanics and Electrician Signals worked in shifts to maintain the equipment, with two on duty in each of the five 'dugouts' at Polygon. Those on duty were also responsible for keeping a 'Log' of the schedules, frequencies, aerials, transmitter performance and required to change frequency and aerials when instructed, via telephone, by operators at GHQ.

Polygon Wireless Station was expanding rapidly during 1942. All the personal sleeping accommodation (except the officers' quarters) at Polygon was in regulation tents which were about 20 feet (6m) square with 5 foot (1.5m) walls with an access on one side only. They had a canvas roof, supported by a 12 foot (3.6m) vertical central pole which was angled at around 40 degrees between the top of the walls and the pole. Before a new tent could be erected it was necessary to dig a large hole 22 feet (6.7m) square and 4 feet (1.2m) deep, which would provide some protection against shrapnel during air raids.

Part of Army base in desert near Cairo

Sgt R.G. Shears, Cairo, March 1942

Rowley on his Matchless motorcycle

Rowley with 2 colleagues and a newly delivered British Army No.5 set

British Army No. 5 set, HP (High Power)

Rowley in a workshop at Polygon Wireless Station

Rowley with an RCA ET4750 transmitter in Cairo

SIME Authority note for driving WD (War Department) vehicles

Lieut. R.G. Shears in desert uniform

Rowley in the JCJC Studio (Polygon Wireless Station)

Chapter 17
JCJC Broadcasting Services for the Troops in Egypt (1942–1944)

Rowley had many meetings in the Company Office with Major Charles Kidd, together with other GHQ Signals officers, where they discussed operational requirements such as time schedules, allocation of the transmitters and use of directional aerials. It was at one of these meetings when Rowley suggested to the Major that perhaps, subject to GHQ Senior Officers' approval, they could use one of the 7.5 kW (RCA ET-4750) transmitters, which was normally only in use at night for high-speed telegraphy, to start up a local Forces Broadcasting Service for a few hours in the daytime. The current radio entertainment offering for the troops was very limited and Rowley had maintained his early interest in broadcasting radio and music. The Major and the officers were enthusiastic about the idea and thought that a strong signal could be provided to the Western Desert, Cyprus, Palestine, Sudan, Syria and Persia. The Major agreed to see Brigadier Eric Cole DCSO (Deputy Chief Signals Officer), who'd been on Rowley's Officers Selection Board, to seek his approval. They then made a list of the requirements which included finding some space for a studio, as well as sourcing music amplifiers, turntables, audio mixer and a large supply of records. Rowley thought he could source some of the equipment needed from his contacts at the BBC studio in Cairo and also from his friend Norman Joly (SV1RX) who worked with the Egyptian State Broadcasting service.

Major Kidd spoke to the Brigadier and to senior officers in the RAF and Royal Navy, "instilling enthusiasm for the idea of daily forces broadcasts" and they offered their support. Rowley says he got to know the Major quite well during this time and admired his ability to "cut red tape" and "get things done". Rowley notes that it only took about ten days for Charles to receive the go-ahead for the Forces Broadcasting Station on a trial basis. As expected, there were certain conditions under which the service could operate, and these were:

- Broadcasts to be restricted to musical entertainment from gramophone records.
- Only commentary to be Station identity and programme announcements.
- Station identity to be "This is a test transmission from the British Army Station JCJC transmitting on a frequency of 7220 kilocycles[1] in the 41-metre band".
- There must be no mention of 'British Forces Network' or 'BFN'.
- No extra staff to be enlisted for the project.

Charles and Rowley were happy to agree to the terms and a reply letter was immediately sent confirming their agreement. The call sign, JCJC, was the same as that used on all 'high speed telegraphy' traffic emanating from, or direct to, GHQ Cairo. All Signals stations on the circuits had their own call signs, for example London was JLJL and Delhi, JDJD.

Once they had the official approval, they started to collect the necessary equipment and, with Major Charles' agreement, they decided to set up the studio in an unused area of the south dugout, furthest from the transmitters. Several personnel volunteered to help with the set-up during their off-duty hours. These included carpenters, 'Electrician Signals' and a lance corporal who had worked in the maintenance department of BBC studios before the war. Within a couple of weeks, the room was beginning to resemble a studio with boards installed on the walls to deaden the sound, and

---
[1] Kilocycles – short for kilocycles per second (kc/s) in use at the time. Unit of frequency, denoting one thousand cycles per second. Now replaced by kilohertz, kHz.

a control desk, based on Rowley's sketches, was built to house record turntables, microphones and other equipment. Once cabling was added to connect all the equipment together, they were then ready for testing. Rowley notes that they had a few teething problems as the mix of equipment loaned to them was from many countries and didn't necessarily work together as expected. Meanwhile Major Charles had been collecting a variety of '78' records, some donated and some loaned, which all had to be labelled and catalogued. Charles asked his girlfriend, 'Trish' (Patricia), who later became his wife after repatriation to the UK in 1945, to help with this. Like Anne, she was a Junior Commander in the ATS and was the Officer-in-charge of the largest military telephone exchange in the Middle East, TME (Telecommunications Middle East).

Once the JCJC studio equipment had all been checked and a screened audio cable had been run from the studio to the RCA ET-4750 transmitter, they were ready for the first 'on-air' test transmission. After exchanging messages with the Abwehr on a Saturday evening, Rowley met two sergeants just coming off duty and asked them if they could help with the 'air test' the following morning in the south dugout, which they agreed to. Once the overnight traffic had been cleared at the Signals Office, Rowley had asked the duty Signals officer at the dugout to close down the transmitter. This was to allow it to cool before he made a few changes to the aerial feeders and various metal straps and switches inside the transmitter housing so that he could re-tune to the frequency of 7220 kilocycles (7.22 MHz) which had been allocated for the new service. They also needed to connect the new aerial, which Rowley had designed, and make some circuit changes to switch in the modulator section. The modulator was required because they were going to be using voice and music transmissions. The next morning Rowley had five pairs of hands to help him and between them they made the changes needed. After several trials, which took around four hours and were done in a very manual way as they did not have suitable test equipment, they had achieved full modulation with minimal distortion.

At this point Rowley asked operators at the other four dugouts as well as the Signals office in Grey Pillars, and several other units at Heliopolis and Maadi, to tune to 7220 kilocycles and send a signal report back. All reports were satisfactory including one from Charles who had been listening in the Officers' Mess and then drove over on his motor bike to the south dugout to personally congratulate Rowley and the team. They were now almost ready to start broadcasting and agreed a date for the first broadcast, hoping that they would receive a suitable number of records by then.

Rowley needed a few days to write the procedures for changing the transmitter configuration, to document details of the meter readings on the ET-4750 and to make up a logbook to record transmission times, announcements and records played. It was agreed that broadcasts would run in the afternoon between 14.00 and 17.00. Having found a copy of the Coldstream Guards playing 'Colonel Bogey' in the record collection, Rowley decided to adopt that tune as the station's theme tune which would "open all transmissions".

Wednesday afternoon arrived, and at 13.50 Rowley switched on the transmitter, checked the modulation and at 13.58 started playing the Colonel Bogey record until 14.00 when he announced:

"GOOD AFTERNOON TO ALL LISTENERS – THIS IS A TEST TRANSMISSION FROM BRITISH ARMY STATION JCJC ON A FREQUENCY OF 7220 KILOCYCLES IN THE 41-METRE BAND. WE WILL BE TRANSMITTING DAILY ON THIS FREQUENCY BETWEEN 11.00 AND 14.00 (GREENWICH MEAN TIME) – WE HOPE ALL LISTENERS WILL ENJOY THE PROGRAMMES. NEXT, WE HAVE 'THE BLUE DANUBE' BY STRAUSS."

Rowley had arranged for signal reports from troops in the desert to be received via the Army, Navy and RAF Services Post Office. The broadcasts were continually monitored in the Officers' Mess where his fellow officers were hoping to hear Rowley make a slip of the tongue. They did accuse him on one occasion of introducing the "Coldcream Guards" – it was all a bit of fun! After a few weeks of operating and as the numbers of listeners grew, more records were being received from a variety of places. One large package of records arrived from ENSA (Entertainments National Service Association), in London and there was also an offer from an English lady in Cairo who telephoned Rowley to say how much she was enjoying the music choice. The lady offered to loan her 24 record set (all 78's) of 'Madame Butterfly' by Puccini sung in Italian which Rowley collected from her house in the Gezira area.

Rowley scheduled the Puccini opera broadcast and made radio announcements to advertise it during the week before. On the afternoon of playing this collection, Rowley had assistance from an off duty "organ-playing Signalman" to help with the constant juggling between the two turntables, in order to play each side of a record in the correct sequence. The studio was 20ft below ground and accessed via an open staircase. When Rowley left the dugout to get some fresh air whilst the Puccini opera was playing, he met a dozen or so Italian POWs standing around and straining to hear the music faintly rising from the studio monitor speakers below ground. They had just heard the famous aria 'Ora a Noi' and Rowley commented that he had never seen so many grown men with tears rolling down their cheeks. The music had probably made them feel homesick or perhaps they had simply been starved of beautiful music since landing in North Africa. In unison they said "molte grazie Capitan" and saluted him. Rowley notes the Italians always seemed to elevate the British in the Army by one rank as they already called the corporal in charge of the POWs a sergeant! Before the end of the broadcast Rowley received a phone call from his friend Norman Joly, at Egyptian State Broadcasting, asking if he would like the 'time pips' to be put through the telephone line at the next hour. Rowley accepted the offer and the time pips subsequently became a feature of JCJC Broadcasting Station. Norman had been a radio amateur (call signs SVIRX & G3FNJ) in pre-war Greece and had escaped to Cairo with other British Embassy staff from Athens when the Nazis arrived there in April 1941.

Reports on signal quality in most areas around Cairo were generally good but it became clear that a better signal with less 'fading' was needed for the large audience in the Cairo area. Whilst discussing the results with Major Charles, Rowley suggested they should have a second transmitter which could operate in the medium wave band (simultaneously with the short wave) and get permission to broadcast at that frequency. Fortunately, Rowley had recently acquired a new transmitter in readiness for this purpose and Charles agreed to arrange the frequency allocation. The new transmitter had been loaned by the United States Army. A US sergeant had previously visited Rowley at the radio studio to enquire if he could get a copy of a recording of 'Perfidia' sung in Spanish, which Rowley had played on air. Rowley had loaned him the record and had accepted an invitation to his base, set up in the desert about 20 miles outside of Cairo. Sergeant Nagy's section was providing communications for US units in the Middle East mainly in connection with the new US Airforce landing strip (Bayn or Payne Field Airforce Base) – which later became part of the new Cairo airport. On his visit Rowley enjoyed an introduction "to American goodies" such as peanut butter, doughnuts, cookies and coffee but also got a chance to visit the workshops and stores. Here, he spotted a plentiful supply of Hallicrafters BC610 transmitters and enquired if he could borrow one for his radio broadcasts. Rowley carried out the many modifications to convert the new BC610 to a medium wave frequency. Sgt Nagy supported his endeavours by supplying "a box full of BC610 components", some spare valves/tubes and a handbook with circuit diagrams. Once up and running on the allotted frequency of 1314 kilocycles, the signal reports from the local area showed that he had achieved good all-round reception which was superior to the short-wave transmission.

Work on improving the JCJC broadcasting offering continued for many months and into 1943. In the latter part of 1942, the high volume of activity in the desert meant a considerable increase in radio traffic for Cheese so Rowley had to curtail his broadcasting duties. He discussed this with Major Charles and it was Trish who came up with the idea of asking for volunteers from Telecommunications Middle East (TME) to be interviewed for a part-time job as announcers, in addition to their normal telephone duties. The three of them decided that it would be appropriate that the main part of the interview would utilise the studio with each applicant reading scripts into the microphone during an 'off-air' period.

Rowley set up a loudspeaker in the Company Office where the "selection committee" (which included Major Charles and Rowley together with four others) would monitor each of the applicants. The committee would not meet anyone beforehand to ensure that judging was based solely on voice quality and their performance. Trish had found 13 willing applicants from TME and they were individually interviewed in the studio, before the committee made their decision.

Over the next few days, the four girls selected visited the studio where Rowley gave them tuition on techniques for making the announcements, operating the microphone and turntables and also for maintaining the time-log of all record titles played. After about ten hours' tuition and practice off-air all four seemed competent and confident enough to go live.

Later on, two more TME girls joined the group and the hours of broadcasting were expanded to include an early morning period starting at 07.00 (Cairo time). Rowley calculated that the propagation conditions at this time would provide a greater signal coverage by around 1500 miles, particularly in the westerly direction. In a letter to his parents back home in New Barnet, Rowley asked them to tune to the 41-metre band on an old Radiogram receiver which Rowley had built in 1938. A few weeks later he received a message back from his parents to say that they had managed to hear him at 5am one morning. As his parents hadn't seen him for over three years, he imagined that they would be overjoyed to hear from him.

Once the medium wave transmissions were working well, and a full supporting team was in place, Rowley only did the occasional broadcast session as his Cheese communications and other intelligence activities were prioritised. He did manage to come on air in August 1944 to wish his sister (Dorothy) 'good luck' on the day of her wedding.

The early success of the Cairo radio station was eventually reported in the UK newspapers, but not until 1944. On Saturday the 29th July 1944, the *Daily Mail* newspaper carried an article entitled "1-MAN RADIO SHOWS BBC: No Talk – Troops Happy" from their correspondent in Cairo. It explained that "Somewhere in the Middle East", a British Military Radio Engineer was giving the troops what they wanted to hear on air – "simple entertainment and genuine relaxation". The *Daily Herald* also published a similar article on the same date with their title "This is the Radio our men like". Both reports mentioned the popularity of the station and the large amount of fan mail being sent to the presenter. Rowley noted that for security reasons his name or rank were not divulged. He remained in charge of the JCJC Army Broadcast until October 1944. By then the station had been formerly renamed as 'Forces Broadcasting', and it continued to operate after he left Egypt.

Chapter 18
Prizes for Deception

During the early stages of the JCJC broadcasting period in 1942, Rowley had continued to give Morse practice and message procedure lessons to Anne. There was now some urgency for her to take over some of the radio operating part of Operation Cheese, so, after many weeks of intensive training, tests of Anne's 'fist' were arranged to see if anybody could tell the difference between her messages and Rowley's. The tests were carried out scientifically by Rowley in a random order, with four senior sergeant operators based at Polygon in the Sergeants' Mess listening in on headphones. The sergeants were told that Rowley would be sending the first message, and they needed to identify who was sending the messages that followed. After the tests ended, the consensus was that it was difficult to determine the difference between Anne and Rowley.

Before the test results could finally be decided upon by his Intelligence masters, Rowley had to focus on a series of requests from the Abwehr relating to extremely sensitive information which again might jeopardise the imminent action of Allied troops in the desert. Previously he had faked a breakdown of the transmitter in order to delay a transmission so Rowley was asked if there was another way to affect a sudden break in a message without arousing suspicion. Rowley suggested the use of a 'Q' code, specifically a 'QRR' code, which although not used much anymore, would notify the receiver that there was an emergency or security alert. This would make sense for a spy in Cairo who was surrounded by Allied troops and Military Police and was always expecting a knock on the door whilst he was transmitting, so would probably sound realistic when used. Rowley suggested that they send a message to the Abwehr, questioning their understanding of emergency 'QRR' messages. Major Robertson agreed with this idea and said that this new message could be encoded and sent along with an evasive reply to the Abwehr request for information on armaments carried on the latest versions of A30 Cruiser tanks. These Cruiser tanks were fast and well-armed tanks which were able to fight enemy tanks, particularly on open ground.

Expecting to start the contact at 8pm with a new call sign and then wait for a reply, Rowley was surprised to hear the Abwehr contacting him first using both his new call sign and theirs. He immediately recognised the fist of 'Wolfgang', whom he believed to be the officer in charge of their Signals Office, and they started to exchange messages. After confirming that he was ready to receive the first message, Rowley noted down Wolfgang's message on his pad of paper. Rowley then sent his two messages and at the end of the second message included the clue for the next message which related to the next starting point in the Gone with the Wind book. During the short time that Rowley was sending these two messages Captain McKenzie, Rowley's line officer, was decoding Wolfgang's message to them. As Rowley terminated the transmission, Captain McKenzie became quite excited, commenting that the message appeared to be something special and "more or less of a personal nature – no wonder the officer in charge wanted to send it to you".

Rowley helped him to finish the decoding and translation of the message. It read:

"WE WISH TO INFORM YOU THAT THE FÜHRER HAS BEEN PLEASED TO AWARD YOU THE IRON CROSS FOR SERVICES TO THE VATERLAND. HE HOPES TO CONGRATULATE YOU PERSONALLY WHEN YOU RETURN TO BERLIN – HH. *(Heil Hitler).*

THE MEDAL WILL BE SENT TO YOU BY COURIER SERVICE – THE SAME ROUTE AS BEFORE WHEN FUNDS WERE SENT. GOOD LUCK."

A few days later Rowley was summoned to the SIME office of Brigadier Maunsell, who congratulated him and agreed that the medal would be presented to him when it arrived, as he had spent so much time and shown great skill in maintaining his assignment. Brigadier Maunsell wished Rowley 'good luck' as he left.

Although many enquiries were made of the package containing his medal it was never found. Through diplomatic channels, SIME were advised that a package had arrived in Istanbul, and then Beirut, Haifa and Kantara but it did not arrive at the address in Heliopolis. Rowley assumed it had been lost or stolen but there was also the possibility that somebody had decided that it was inappropriate for him to receive such an award!

Rowley was eventually presented with a second-class Iron Cross when, many years later, his youngest son Jeremy gave him one as a birthday present, having purchased it from a London dealer in medals and rare coins.

Rowley noted that the award was not the end of Operation Cheese and that in fact he became even more involved.

Chapter 19
'A' Force Cairo

Whilst working with SIME, and on regular visits to them in Grey Pillars in Cairo, Rowley came into contact with a small group of imaginative and creative deceptionists who were part of 'A' Force Cairo, a department within SIS (Secret Intelligence Service) (MI6) with direct reporting lines to the Cairo-based Commander-in-Chief Middle East (Wavell then Auchinleck) and also to Prime Minister, Winston Churchill, in London. The group had been recruited by Lt. Colonel Dudley Clarke and members had been chosen for their sometimes 'quirky' individual talents. Some came from the military; others were civilians from various walks of life.

Rowley notes that he knew a major, possibly Victor Jones – one of three majors originally working with Dudley Clarke, who was in command of a large workshop in the Alexandria area and who frequently visited the SIME offices. He later learned that this major's company was involved in making dozens of dummy tanks, vehicles, and artillery out of cardboard and plywood. They were designed to look exactly the same as the real machinery (shape, colour, artwork and desert grey camouflage), especially when viewed from a distance. This deception was to have a major impact in the final battle for El Alamein.

Dudley Clarke, who is now known as the Chief of Deception operations in Africa during WWII, also helped to create 1st Special Air Service Brigade, a forerunner to the Special Air Services (SAS).

In early 1941, 'A' Force was just a handful of officers and later, at maximum strength, it still only consisted of some 41 officers and 76 NCOs. It worked closely with SIME, so Rowley would have been part of their operations as they utilised the success of 'Cheese' to send misinformation. Rowley worked with 'A' Force, under Dudley

Clarke's command, from Autumn 1941 and it was Dudley Clarke who recommended him for a British Empire Medal (BEM) in early 1943. In his recommendation, Colonel Dudley Clarke stated that Rowley's "most highly secret work" for the organisation under Dudley Clarke's control (for 18 months since Autumn 1941), had been conducted in his own off duty time, and by 1942 this involved two to three hours nightly for six days a week.

Chapter 20
Operation Wild Goose – A New German Agent

In June 1942 the Allies had lost control of Tobruk and Rommel was at his strongest. There was a degree of confidence about the success of the German campaign, and they were expecting to be in Cairo soon.

The Abwehr had previously informed Rowley that they were moving part of their radio station transmissions from Sofia to Athens and Rowley noted that five of the original operators, including 'Wolfgang', had now arrived there. Rowley had noticed, over recent months, that some operators had not been heard from and that several newcomers had arrived. These newcomers were all very good Morse operators and as they became regulars, he added them to his list of operators. Contact schedules remained at two to three times per week and Anne sat in on these so that she could become familiar with the different operators and read the Morse through the various forms of interference which were frequently present. Sometimes when the interference was bad Rowley had to request that parts of the five letter groups be repeated to ensure that they were received correctly. When the signals were too weak to read at all, the transmission was re-scheduled for another time, either later that day or the next day. In contrast, Rowley was aware that the Abwehr had very powerful military transmitters and receivers as well as more efficient aerials. This meant that they very rarely asked him to repeat anything which he sent.

Within two days of sending the message regarding the 'QRR' code, Rowley had received confirmation from the Abwehr that they recognised it as a security alert and on receipt would tell all their operators to report it to the Officer Superintendent. Rowley discussed this with Major Robertson on his next visit and was told that they might need to use this code soon, as the requests for information about 8th Army movements (at this time retreating towards El Alamein) were very sensitive. The plan was to answer them as fully as possible but only at the appropriate time. Over the next two or three weeks, messages and requests for information about desert troop movements were averaging about four per week. There were continual requests for information about Allied desert troop movements within a triangular area from El Alamein to the Qattara Depression and El Hamman on the Mediterranean coast. They also asked for information about convoys arriving in the Suez Canal zone, particularly the numbers of Air Force personnel, aircraft types and the countries involved. Answering these questions provided a lot of work for the intelligence gathering team at SIME. That SIME work was then analysed by senior staff at Headquarters Middle East, who consulted Army and sometimes Air Force staff as appropriate, before approving small sections of the intelligence for encoding and transmission.

Rowley noted that as the Abwehr had moved part of their radio station to the Athens area this would necessitate a change of frequency because of the shorter signal path. Call signs and time schedules were also changed. He made the necessary changes and monitored the new frequency for a few nights, noting that it was free of interference.

'Wolfgang', having moved to the new location, had put in an appearance during the discussions about the frequency changes. This time there were no extra messages about potential air raids, so Rowley wondered if he wasn't privy to this information anymore. When, ten days later, a message came through from him, Rowley wondered whether it would be especially significant again. The confidence of the Germans was apparent in his next message which was decoded by Rowley, Anne and Captain Desmond Doran from SIME, whom Rowley notes was "killed later (1946) whilst staying at Hotel St David in Jerusalem, when it was blown up by Palestinian Patriots".

The message read:

"MILITARY SITUATION IN DESERT CAMPAIGN HAS IMPROVED.
WE REQUIRE YOUR EXPERT ATTENTION IN ALEXANDRIA.
PLEASE GO THERE TO SELECT ACCOMMODATION READY TO CONTINUE OPERATION.
RETURN TO CAIRO AND SEND YOUR REPORT IN 3/5 DAYS."
"ARRANGEMENTS MADE FOR NEW AGENT TO ARRIVE EGYPT WITH TWO SMALL TRANSMITTER/RECEIVERS AND FUNDS ETC IN APPROX 14 DAYS FROM THIS DATE.
WE WANT YOU TO MEET AND ADVISE HIM.
DETAILS TO FOLLOW.
PLEASE OBSERVE TOTAL SECURITY AS ALWAYS."

Rowley notes that he attended a meeting at Grey Pillars the day after receiving the message at which they discussed the various aspects of meeting the new agent, some of which were hypothetical until the true facts were clearer. There was a concern about who would take over the radio operating (posing as the new agent, once he was captured) in Alexandria as Rowley already had enough commitments operating 'Cheese' back in Cairo. Rowley advised that he couldn't manage this new agent as well as Cheese communications from Alexandria as the Abwehr could identify that the Cheese messages were not originating from Cairo as expected. Afterwards, Major Robertson sent one of their colleagues to the SIME office in Alexandria to inform them of this development and Rowley made his way back to the Polygon Wireless Station in Abbassieh.

Once back in his workshop at Polygon, he noted that he was surprised to hear a message for him at the scheduled time that evening, from one of the new Abwehr operators, which could have been a "trick". He didn't answer the message that night as he was supposed to be in Alexandria, looking for suitable accommodation.

Rowley was ready to send a message the next evening to say that suitable secure accommodation had been found in Alexandria, but there were no calls from the Abwehr and his three calls went unanswered. All signals were very, very weak at this time and there appeared to be a partial black-out of all short-wave signals which was affecting all communications to and from Polygon. Rowley notes that this black-out of short-wave signals was known as the "Dellinger Effect" and was related to a disturbance of the earth's atmosphere caused by solar flares on the sun. One day later, once conditions had improved, Rowley sent an encoded message to confirm that "accommodation had been found in Alexandria". He told them that the new location would be referred to as "Etneen" (number 2) and his existing base as "Wahed" (number 1).

The Abwehr response read:

"DETAILS OF NEW AGENT NOT YET AVAILABLE.
REQUEST YOU BE PREPARED AT 24 HOURS NOTICE TO MEET, POSSIBLY IN AN AREA SIMILAR TO YOUR 'OWN' ARRIVAL.
TAKE A VEHICLE.
WE WILL CALL YOU DAILY AT AGREED TIME AND FREQUENCY.
WHEN INFORMATION IS SENT IT WILL BE BY SYSTEM-X. ACKNOWLEDGE THIS MESSAGE IS UNDERSTOOD IN ONE HOUR."

System-X was a more elaborate method of encoding devised by the Abwehr for top security messages. It was more time consuming to use as it required three transpositions of letters to be applied instead of the normal two.

Rowley, Anne and Guy Thompson, from SIME, who was with Rowley that evening, decided on the reply to be sent and had it encoded within the hour so that it could be sent on time. Rowley responded:

> "RECEIVED AND UNDERSTOOD, PLEASE GIVE NAME OF AGENT OR CODE NAME WHEN REPLYING."

Rowley noted the air of anticipation and excitement as he met with Major Robertson, Major Thompson, Captain Doran and Brigadier Maunsell (who stayed for half an hour before going on to another meeting) at Grey Pillars the next day. All at the meeting agreed that the apparent success of the Cheese operation meant that the Abwehr were preparing to send another agent via the same route, and delivery method, that they had used for Alex. He had been put ashore in a dinghy by the German Navy on a lonely beach in the Nile Delta but was not arrested until he reached Cairo. Major Robertson advised them that he was already going through the 'Alex interrogation' reports prepared by 'Major Max' in anticipation of a repeat performance. Rowley notes that Major Max, who was an international class tennis player and performed well at the pre-war Olympics, was a brilliant linguist and a tough interrogator. Rowley had witnessed him on two occasions when he was extracting information from Alex.

They had to assume that the new agent, who was expecting to meet Alex, would have a photograph of him and they needed somebody of a similar stature who was fluent in German, preferably with a Berliner accent, to play the part. Major Robertson identified somebody who could "fit the bill", a Captain Arnold Klosser of Force 133 (SOE Cairo), although he thought he might be sailing on a fishing boat around the Greek islands in pursuit of information.

A plan was hatched for up to a dozen undercover armed infantry to support Captain Klosser (or an alternative SIME officer) with the initial meeting and for Rowley and Major Thompson to be stationed in a small town called El Hamul, about 15km from the coast. The supporting infantry would stay at the Egyptian Army barracks in the same town.

The Royal Navy Intelligence in Alexandria had already been informed and they were ready to offer RN assistance as required. Rowley notes that he planned to borrow two of the latest US Signals portable transmitter/receiver units from his friend (Sergeant Nagy) in the US Signals detachment. This would be used to provide wireless links between the coast (meeting party) and El Hamul. Rowley borrowed the equipment, explaining that it was needed for three to four weeks to test the prospect of providing a wireless link between Polygon and the Dead City station. He tested it for the next week between the American base and his own workshop at Polygon. After that, he was confident that it was suitable for the operation.

Rowley maintained contact with the Abwehr, calling every evening at the appointed time, but no messages were received from them. After waiting a week, the Abwehr advised of a seven to ten day delay but after this, finally, the long-awaited message was received from 'Wolfgang'. After decoding, it read:

"OPERATION – WILD GOOSE – DATE – SUNDAY 2nd AUGUST 1942
TIME 00:30 GMT.
MEET CODE NAME XXXX.
ARRIVAL ONE KM EAST OF MASYAF BALTIM ON SEASHORE.
IDENTITY SIGNAL BY BEAM TORCH LIGHT THREE MORSE DASHES *(letter O)* AT INTERVALS TO/FROM BOTH PARTY TO ESTABLISH CONTACT. KEEP VEHICLE NEAR VENUE.

OBSERVE MAXIMUM SECURITY.
RETURN TO YOUR BASE ON COMPLETION OF OPERATION.
REPORT AT NEXT SCHEDULED TIME.
GOOD LUCK.
END OF MESSAGE."

The following night, Rowley enquired about any alternative arrangements should there be an unexpected delay and he could not make contact with the new agent. The reply advised that if operation 'Wild Goose' was unsuccessful on the given date it would be delayed for an unspecified period.

Rowley and his colleagues only had four days in which to finalise their plans and ensure that everybody involved understood their role. Rowley was involved in numerous meetings; special maps were issued and wireless links were installed. As it was assumed that a vessel or two from the German Navy would be involved, SIME officers had several meetings with senior officers of the Royal Navy where they put emphasis on getting the agent safely ashore. After that, the Navy could take whatever action they thought was necessary.

Rowley had made arrangements to have one of the wireless units (borrowed from the US Signal Corps) installed into a vehicle with a whip aerial so that it could be operated whilst mobile. He headed to El Hamul early the next morning in that vehicle and met up with two Intelligence Corps Staff Sergeants who had the other wireless set and aerial in their staff car. The group of three met up with Guy Thompson and another SIME officer in the fishing village of Masyaf Baltim and they found a storage building overlooking the small port where they set up and tested the equipment. They then walked two to three kilometres along pathways which were probably only visited by ornithologists observing the wildlife, to the designated landing beach. This proved to be a very unattractive, dirty and lonely beach area, nothing like Alexandria's sandy beaches. Apparently, the

German Navy had used this area before for putting spies ashore as it (according to the Royal Navy) offered a safe stable anchorage about 1km offshore. Rowley left his vehicle and equipment in the care of the local police at El Hamul police station and travelled back with Guy to Polygon in good time for his evening schedule, where the messaging confirmed that he was going to be kept busy for the next four or five nights.

On the Friday, a further exchange of messages with the Abwehr took place in which the Germans confirmed that 'Operation Wild Goose' was on schedule with the landing due early morning on the following Sunday. On Saturday, Rowley put on his civilian clothes and packed a few essentials in a bag he had bought at the 'Muski market' (Cairo's Souk). He was prepared for overnight stays in case the operation got delayed. With Guy driving, they headed north out of Cairo to El Hamul, a 70 mile journey which took over two hours as the roads were in an awful condition. That evening they met with all the other agencies in a private room of a hotel, where the proprietor had been told they were on a training exercise. They planned for everybody to take up their positions within an hour after midnight. After this, Rowley, Guy and the Infantry Company Sergeant Major drove to the coast and the port to check the wireless links then went back to the hotel, to get ready for the operation. The team took up their positions, some at the port and some on the beach. Rowley notes that it was a warm night with quite a lot of cloud, some patches of clear sky and a slight breeze – ideal conditions for the operation.

As midnight approached there was a great feeling of expectation with all watching for the expected signals from out at sea. The SIME 'forward' man was on the deserted part of the beach, with his torch at the ready, to respond to the "three long dashes" beamed from a powerful torch, when it came. Unless things went wrong, the SIME man acting as Alex was to be the only man on the beach. At 03.35 local time an observer thought he saw a faint light a long way out to sea and several more of these lights were reported to the control centre over the next half hour. The team did not believe that these lights were from fishing boats as they had been told that the fishing boat crews had a holiday until 04.00 am on Monday morning. By daybreak, nothing had happened and it was thought that a 24-hour delay might have occurred. The reception party and observers at the port remained on alert.

Later that day, as soon as they were able to establish communications with the SIME office from the hotel, Rowley and Guy learnt that the Royal Navy had informed them that the operation was all off. They were all concerned about the Royal Navy message and their change of plan. Rowley notes that there was nothing more for them to do though, so they thanked all the team, packed up all the equipment and headed back to their various quarters for some sleep! Rowley collected his vehicle and drove to the port at Masyaf Baltim to collect the other radio transmitter/receiver.

Driving back to Abbassieh, Rowley spent time thinking about his next message to the Abwehr. As an agent, Rowley would want to know why the new agent had not arrived and would also need to confirm that he had been at the reception point at the correct time and had waited until dawn. To make it even more convincing, Rowley would also show his willingness to return to the beach again in a few hours' time in case 'Operation Wild Goose' was being rescheduled after a delay.

At a meeting at Grey Pillars on the Monday, the SIME team agreed the format of the next message to confirm that the agent had not arrived and it was encoded for transmission to the Abwehr that evening. The Abwehr had no news about the delay of 'Operation Wild Goose'.

Meanwhile, a coded message had come through to SIME at Grey Pillars from their team in Alexandria who had been liaising with the Royal Navy Intelligence Office. The message stated that "the Royal Navy were escorting a U-boat and its crew to Alexandria, but there is no news yet about your chap. The Navy in Alexandria are elated

– sorry for your disappointment. Further information will follow as soon as possible after de-briefing session. Royal Navy destroyer with vessel being escorted, expected alongside dock at 09.00 tomorrow".

There was much conjecture in the SIME camp as to why the Navy's action deviated from the original plan.

Back at Grey Pillars again the next day, Rowley was informed that the Royal Navy had the U-boat secured in a top security pen in Alexandria and there appeared to be some damage to the "conning tower". The commander and crew had been sent to various interrogation centres and there had been one civilian on board (although he was dressed in naval uniform), who had been in possession of a small transmitter/receiver and several encoding/coding documents. An agreement was reached between SIME and Naval Intelligence to release "the civilian" into SIME's care on completion of the Navy's interrogation, and for Rowley to examine the wireless transmitter/receiver but Rowley notes this did not happen.

A few days later the 'U-boat' commander had admitted that his vessel had been attacked by aircraft. They had experienced problems with their radio equipment which left them unable to contact either of their bases in Germany and Italy, or the German-held ports in north Africa or the supply ship. The Navy had changed the original plan to take advantage of the situation presented to them and although disappointed, those at the SIME office agreed that it had been a very successful Naval operation.

Rowley notes that he was told that much useful naval intelligence was gathered from the crew of the captured U-boat and Brigadier Maunsell felt optimistic that the man they were expecting would be handed over to SIME within a week or so.

It was not until three months later that the Germans made an announcement about the loss of the submarine in one of their regular radio broadcasts, that usually only boasted of Hitler's successes. The broadcast, which was picked up by an Allied listening station based at Nathanya (Netanya) in Palestine, said that "they regretted to announce the probable loss of U-boat 372, believed to be due to enemy action in the Mediterranean".

Chapter 21

The Gezira Project – The Spy and The Sabotage Expert

In late summer 1942, the British 8th Army was now under the command of General Bernard Law Montgomery (nicknamed 'Monty'). Rommel and his troops had established themselves along a line south-west from El Alamein and had apparently been receiving intelligence reports that British, Australian and New Zealand forces were amassing east of El Alamein and to the south. Reinforcements were also arriving in large quantities on ships in the Suez Canal area. This led to an increase of Abwehr messages (five or six days a week) and questions for information on regiments, corps, RAF personnel and armaments. Rowley notes they always made a practice of replying to all questions and that much misleading information was passed to the Abwehr during this time. Some questions took up to three weeks to be responded to due to the complexity of the requests.

As Anne had become quite proficient and was able to handle the majority of the radio traffic at this time, Major Robertson saw an opportunity to get Rowley involved in some other projects and invited him to meet an intelligence officer, Captain George D. Klingopolis, and "some of his friends", who were based on Gezira Island in Cairo. The island is situated just off the west bank of the River Nile and is connected to land by a causeway.

As they drove onto the island in Major Robertson's staff car, Rowley observed several large and very smart villas, one of which had a couple of poles and wireless aerials on, marking it out as their destination. During the short drive to the meeting, Major Robertson had explained that in addition to the staff and armed guards, the island had facilities for four or five detainees, and they had five there at present. All of these detainees had been picked up by the Military Police in Cairo and found to have wireless transmitters and encoding/decoding information, either with them or hidden in various locations. During the previous few months, they had been interrogated and detained in prison, but having agreed to cooperate they had now been transferred to SIME and the Gezira establishment. Each one of them had been placed in the charge of a SIME officer who spoke their language.

As they entered the villa with the radio equipment, they were met by Captain Klingopolis who showed them the wireless equipment, the interview room and the library, which was equipped with both English and foreign language books as well as puzzles and games. The setting was very informal and relaxing which was intentional. Captain Klingopolis, known as 'Kling', explained that he had played chess with his detainee and discussions between them during those games had given him an insight into his family background and his political interests. Kling said they would refer to the detainee as 'Nicolas', adding that he knew the English joke about this name meaning 'copper bottom'!

Major Robertson, Kling and Rowley sat down to discuss how they could obtain valuable information for SIME by sending encoded messages to the Abwehr via the detainees. Could they be trusted and would the Abwehr still be monitoring the allocated frequencies after a lapse of several months since the detainees had stopped transmitting? Rowley suggested that the first step in the process would be to check the impounded equipment and Major Robertson confirmed that this was why they needed Rowley there and asked him if he could do the checks on Gezira Island. It was agreed that Kling would get the list of frequencies and schedules, and Rowley would start the next day.

On their way back to GHQ, Rowley was updated on the other detainees held at the island. Their nationalities were Greek, Italian, Bulgarian and a Yugoslav. As part of this project, Major Robertson advised Rowley to wear civilian clothes on informal visits and always to carry his 'green pass'. He also explained that he did not want Rowley to meet with Nicolas at this early stage, the reason for this becoming clearer later.

The next morning at the 'radio villa' Rowley started to look at the equipment which Kling had arranged on a table in a room adjacent to the one they had met in yesterday. This room had the terminations for the two outside aerials, brought in through the windows. Rowley recognised the equipment in the room, the first piece being a short-wave communications receiver manufactured by Eddystone Radio of Birmingham. Apparently, this was one of six sets of the same equipment which had been 'borrowed' from 3 GHQ Signals, having been consigned from the UK for use in the Signals Office. He plugged in the receiver, connected one of the aerials and tested it by listening to several Morse transmissions.

He was back again the next morning and arrived as Kling was unpacking some equipment. Rowley was passed a cardboard box which contained the transmitter/receiver found in the possession of Nicolas when he was arrested. The transmitter with receiver and the Morse key were in a leather case with a handle, which reminded Rowley of the British designed and manufactured 'B2' set which had been successfully used by Allied agents in occupied Europe for the past two years. This unit was, however, smaller and lighter than the 'B2' and was of Italian origin. Rowley notes that the units inside the case were stylish and beautifully designed. There was no indication of model numbers but 'TR120(MM)' was stamped on the chassis and Rowley expected it had been made by Magneti Marelli in Milan. Along with the transmitter/receiver were operating sheets printed in German and Italian with handwritten Greek translations on the reverse.

Over the next four or five days, Rowley visited the island each day and conducted his review of the equipment, making copious notes about each piece. Whilst Rowley was doing this, Kling was practising coding and encoding of messages and continuing to have friendly discussions with Nicolas to promote confidence between them. Rowley became aware that Nicolas was receiving favourable treatment as he was receiving a small weekly allowance enabling him to buy things such as soap, fruit, ice cream and chocolate, which Kling arranged to be delivered to him.

Some of the information from their exchanges was passed to Rowley by Kling, enabling him to monitor certain frequencies and observe whether the Abwehr were calling him at all at the given schedule times, using the equipment that Nicolas had arrived with. After monitoring for ten days and, mostly during the evenings, Rowley picked up a weak signal at the scheduled time from the Abwehr calling CBBL which was the call sign allocated to Nicolas. He realised that the aerial he was using was not suitable, so he also erected a further outside aerial to suit the frequency required and provide the best connection possible to an Abwehr station in Athens or Sophia. This construction, which involved making and erecting a dipole between the house and a tree, required a trip to Cairo to purchase lighting cable from an electrical store. That evening the strength of the signal had dramatically improved, and this was reported to Kling and Major Robertson, who both wanted to be present for the next scheduled contact time. Although he hadn't been directly told, Rowley assumed his next role would be to monitor the Morse code and transmissions, with Nicolas operating his own set. In anticipation he had already installed an emergency cut-off button, under his desk, next to the one which Nicolas would use, which would enable him to switch off the transmission, should Nicolas try to warn the Germans.

For his first meeting with Nicolas, Rowley was instructed by Major Robertson to wear his full officer's uniform, including 'Sam Browne' leather belt and shoulder strap instead of his civilian clothes, so Rowley had to return to his officers' quarters, about 10km away, to get changed before returning for the scheduled message time. As he returned to the island, Major Robertson handed him a .38 revolver in a leather holster, and as he fixed it to his 'Sam

Browne', told him to take care as it was loaded! The plan for the evening was for Nicolas to send a message, whilst Rowley listened in on his own receiver, then wait for the Abwehr reply.

Whilst in the canteen for some refreshments, Major Robertson and Kling shared information about Nicolas and his arrival in Egypt. He had been arrested nearly six months ago and, during interrogation by Kling and another Greek-speaking officer, had revealed that he had been a wireless operator at the Greek Embassy in Sofia, Bulgaria. When the German forces had arrived there in 1941, he was detained at Abwehr HQ in Sofia and interrogated by them for several weeks. He had agreed to cooperate with them on the promise that he would be returned to his family in Athens. He had then been sent to the Abwehr training school for secret agents to learn about encoding and decoding of messages as well as signalling procedures. During his training the German Army had advanced quite rapidly into Greece. Eventually he was deposited by U-boat and dinghy onto a secluded Egyptian beach with instructions to make his way to Cairo to meet a Greek Nazi sympathiser who was trusted by the Abwehr. Major Robertson was proud of the fact that it had only taken two weeks after his arrival for him to be captured by SIME and the Military Police. Nicolas had now agreed to become a double agent. Rowley comments that he spoke reasonably good English with a limited vocabulary as well as a "smattering" of essential Arabic words.

Having agreed all the procedures for the evening and checking the equipment, Rowley was wearing headphones and sat behind his Eddystone receiver as the scheduled message time approached. Rowley had been instructed to place his .38 revolver on his desk "to show that you meant business".

Kling brought Nicolas into the room and, conversing in Greek, appeared to explain about Rowley's role before sitting him down at the table opposite Rowley to start the transmission of a prepared message to the Abwehr. As previously agreed, Kling was reminding Nicolas that he must not try to send any warning signal to the

Abwehr, otherwise his future would be severely compromised. Rowley was referred to as a colleague who was a communications expert and thus able to detect any deviation i.e. one extra dot or a longer dash, during the message that was to be sent. Nicolas looked across at Rowley and noted his receiver equipment as well as the revolver on his desk.

Nicolas looked quite nervous as he took the warnings on board. Rowley commented that he looked typically Greek with a medium build, dark hair, brown eyes and a large moustache and was probably in his early thirties. Rowley suggested that he adjust the Morse key to his liking and, when he said he was ready, Rowley was pleased to see that his hand was not shaking and he looked quite composed. He then acknowledged the Abwehr call and invited them to send their message, which consisted of 120 groups of five letters. Both Rowley and Nicolas copied the message down and, as conditions were good, there was no need to ask for any repeats. Nicolas then sent their prepared message with Rowley monitoring each key stroke. The message was without fault but there was a hint of nervousness, which would have seemed quite natural as this was his first message to the Abwehr. Rowley could sense the excitement of the Abwehr operator as he managed to make the first contact with 'their man' and he had to make several corrections in the Morse that he was sending. Two messages were received, and both were taken to the de-ciphering station at GHQ.

Rowley returned to the Radio Villa the next day and on many occasions thereafter. He noted that subsequent messages were without flaws and the Abwehr soon showed confidence in the information being provided to them. The information requested usually related to location of regiments, troops movements and how Nicolas had obtained the information he was providing. Nicolas was sincerely trying to please Kling and Rowley in anticipation of an early release to civilian life as soon as the war ended. His English improved and he asked questions about the possibility of future work in the UK or USA – anywhere but in Germany!

Whilst Rowley and Kling were working with Nicolas, Major Robertson and Kling became involved with another Abwehr agent at Radio Villa who had been detained on Gezira, after being arrested in the Cairo area. Information obtained from this agent indicated that he had lived at an address in Port Said for the six weeks before he was captured. During a raid on those premises by SIME officers and Military Police a collection of explosives including limpet mines were discovered. Under interrogation, this agent (whom Rowley calls "Manfred") admitted that he was an explosives expert and that the explosive devices were specifically designed to destroy parts of metal bridges, tanks, motor vehicles, railway lines and rolling stock.

SIME were initially unsure how the agent was communicating with the Abwehr as they had not found any equipment or coding instructions. A breakthrough occurred when, with the assistance of the Egyptian Telegraph and Telephones company, they were able to track down some regular calls to an apartment in a block of flats in Heliopolis on the outskirts of Cairo. During a search of those premises, a wireless set with aerial wire, some tools and a small book of codes were discovered under the floorboards. These were immediately taken to Major Robertson at Grey Pillars and Rowley was asked to evaluate the equipment whilst Kling and Major Robertson worked on the code book. The wireless set and a small unit, about the size of a cigarette packet, were handed to Rowley, who had never seen anything like it before. This wireless set did not have any tuning knobs or switches which would normally be expected on a receiver. In a compartment at the rear of it, Rowley found a pair of headphones and a socket and a length of cable with a standard two-pin plug, labelled 200-250V. On the front of the box was a knob marked 'Antennenabstimmung' (aerial tuning) and on the top of the box was a terminal marked 'Antenna' and a small pointer knob marked 'F1 and F2'. On the right-hand side of the box was a jack socket marked 'control', which allowed the small cigarette-sized unit to connect to it via a cable.

Rowley observed that the device seemed to be only a transmitter and not a receiver and was keen to know how the agent had been taught to set it up and operate it. He told Major Robertson that this type of equipment was designed to send messages punctually at pre-agreed times and was known as Broadcast Procedure. The receiver of the message could not send any transmission back to the agent. Its operation required a very high level of discipline and punctuality by the agent user who wouldn't easily be able to check that the receiving station were ready to receive the messages he was sending. The small control box was designed to lie flat on a table and had ten parallel slots, (numbered 1, 2, 3, 4, 5, 6, 7, 8, 9, 0), each designed to take the point of a probe. Rowley referred to this as a 'scratch pad box' (a copy of Rowley's sketch of one of these devices is included in the photos section of this book). When inserting the probe into a slot and sliding it downwards, it would make electrical contact with the various copper segments which were different lengths in each slot. The contacts were arranged in a sequence which allowed an operator to send a message in Morse code without them needing to know any Morse code at all. For example, by inserting the probe into the number '5' slot, and sliding the probe downwards, the transmitter would send 5 dots (Morse for number 5) and into the number '7' it would send 2 dashes and 3 dots (Morse for number 7). Predetermined messages could be sent in 4, 5 or 6 figure groups selected from the agent's catalogue of ready-made messages. Major Robertson commented that they had only found a few pages of codes so there must be a full catalogue somewhere. Rowley commented to Major Robertson that he knew of the existence of a Russian catalogue of 4, 5 and 6 figure numbers which had been designed in the 18th century to convey specific instructions, but that the full catalogue was far too big to take into battle as it had over half a million variations. He believed that the Germans had acquired a version of this system and tested it in WWI. It seemed likely that the Abwehr had defined a much smaller selection of specific messages to be used by their operator in Cairo.

Rowley advised that, unlike Morse code, this scratch pad system would not allow for any individuality of the operator, apart from speed or slowness, but the agent had probably been taught to operate at a certain speed when sending a message. Manfred told them he had been taught to send his numerical identity signal '73 73 73 73', before any message by means of his scratch pad. Then this group of numbers would be repeated several times with a three second gap between each group. The agent had confirmed that up to four Abwehr listening stations were primed to listen out for any of his messages.

Rowley was then asked to set up the equipment (without an aerial to avoid full transmission) and to test the system. Once he was happy with this, arrangements were made to bring the agent into the room where Rowley tested all the confiscated equipment, now known as the 'Repair Shop', to allow Manfred to demonstrate his use of the scratch pad to Kling and Major Robertson. Rowley had concocted a message of twenty groups of five figures for Manfred to send. Rowley retired to the adjacent room where he could monitor the transmission through his receiver using headphones and to avoid Manfred having any visual contact with him. This test proved a success, and it was decided that Manfred should be asked to attempt contact with the Abwehr.

Things were now going well for the Allies in the desert and the Abwehr would be keen to hear how their 'sabotage' agent was disrupting the Allies' preparations for advancing in the forthcoming battle of El Alamein. It was agreed that a message would be sent in three days' time, followed by two or three more over the coming two weeks, in order to give the Abwehr false security that their agent was operating as expected. Rowley was asked to be available at short notice to supervise the equipment and monitor the messages. Manfred was told about the message being prepared and provided the details of times at which he was told to send a message on that particular day. These times were either 16:42 or 18:23 GMT (Greenwich Mean Time) and the agent had been told not to use both times and to check his watch each day against the BBC Overseas Service time signal. Rowley selected the later time as the best option for the most favourable propagation conditions and was ready and waiting in his monitoring room as a SIME staff sergeant, armed with a .38 revolver worn in his holster, escorted Manfred into the 'Repair Shop' where Kling was waiting. The armed staff sergeant stood behind Manfred as he sat in front of the equipment and Kling went through the operating procedure with him and reminded him that his messaging was being monitored in the next room.

The first message went well and, confident about the lack of interference at the scheduled time, Rowley was sure that it would have been received by the Abwehr. Three further messages via this method were sent over the next two weeks.

Chapter 22

Back to Cheese in Advance of the Battle for El Alamein

The increased activity around the front at El Alamein brought with it an increase in traffic for 'Cheese'. Anne had been coping well with the traffic but was due some leave and had booked some time in Alexandria for a change of scene. Brigadier Maunsell asked Rowley if he would take it over again as there were now daily questions coming in from the Abwehr who, aware of the build-up on the front, were desperate to learn the positions of artillery, infantry and tanks. The overriding request was "can you find out when and where the enemy will attack?"

As Rowley had previously noted, one of the greatest guises in the El Alamein campaign came at this timepoint. This involved the use of authentic-looking dummy tanks, vehicles and artillery all made from plywood and cardboard which were positioned along the El Alamein lines and designed to look like the real thing when viewed from the air or through binoculars scanning the desert. After the battle of El Alamein, Rowley learnt how the deception had worked. During the week before the advance of the 8th Army troops from the El Alamein lines, when the October nights were cloudy and dark, the armoured tanks and vehicles were moved from their positions to more favourable positions five or six miles away and the dummies were deployed to the area which they had vacated. The ruse worked and the extra activity was noted by Rommel's men.

Rowley (Cheese) received a message from the Abwehr at this time stating that Rommel's HQ had reported many troop movements and requested him to put in maximum effort into obtaining field intelligence on 8th Army movements. He was also asked to increase his transmitting schedules to 06:00, 10:00 and 16:00 hrs local time in case information about the start of the attack became available. Rowley replied that the increased activity and security was making it difficult for his 'contact' in the El Alamein area to communicate with him, but he was giving his full attention to the task.

Two days later Brigadier Raymund Maunsell, the head of SIME, called an urgent meeting of senior staff, including Rowley, in a top security room at Grey Pillars. Maunsell said that he had come from the highest-level meeting with the Commander-in-Chief Middle East, G Ops and RAF where it was announced that "Monty was now ready to start the 'big push' to drive Rommel out of Africa. Subject to suitable weather conditions this would start at 04.00 hrs tomorrow". The Brigadier asked Major Robertson whether this would be the final chapter for Cheese and Major Robertson replied that the larger Cheese network might be ending but as the Abwehr still had total confidence in Rowley's messages, that part of the project would probably continue. Brigadier Maunsell asked whether they should send Abwehr details and time of the impending operation and it was agreed that a message would be encoded and dated for that day then sent at 06.00 hrs tomorrow after the operation had started. Rowley duly sent the message the next day at 06.00 and it was immediately acknowledged by the Abwehr.

Chapter 23
Post Battle of El Alamein and into 1943

Any doubt about whether there would still be regular contact from the Abwehr after this point was dispelled five days after the start of the battle of El Alamein (end October 1942) when they made contact with Rowley enquiring about the health of 'their man' and passing on their thanks for the most helpful information over the past five weeks and for keeping to the schedules. They also made an enquiry about his ability to carry out further work "on behalf of the Reich".

The situation in North Africa was changing very rapidly at this time. American troops had joined other Allied forces and made successful landings in North Africa during November 1942 (Operation Torch), shortly after the Battle of El Alamein. The Abwehr still wanted information about Allied troop (Army, Navy and Airforce) and armament movements and whether these movements were to support the 8th Army or whether they were now moving to other areas.

The German army had now been pushed back out of Egypt to Libya and Tunisia and Rowley notes that there was not a lot to report about supplies to the 8th Army over the next few months (end 1942 and early 1943) as it soon became possible for convoys to get through to North Africa easily via Malta to Tobruk, Bengasi and Alexandria. This saved five to six weeks travelling around the tip of South Africa, up to the Suez Canal and onto Port Tawfiq (Taofik) and Port Said. He sent several messages over this time period to report that he needed to change his location for security reasons and asked for more funds to support his work. The initial response from the Abwehr agreed to arrange this via the special courier route used previously but later they reported that their communications office had been moved to Athens, so they needed to explore another courier method.

Rommel surrendered in May 1943. Once this happened, the Abwehr began to ask Rowley to be on alert for 8th Army troop build-ups in Egypt which might suggest an invasion of Crete and other Greek islands or mainland Greece.

Rowley and Anne continued to provide information, much of it misinformation, which contributed to the false impression that the Allies were planning to launch invasions anywhere other than Sicily or Italy! Similar misinformation and deception operations were planned elsewhere, with a prime example being 'Operation Mincemeat' when a dead body, carrying genuine-looking but fake invasion plans, was planted off the coast of Spain.

With less activity in the Middle East to report to the Abwehr, Rowley spent more time on his Signals day job. He stayed with his unit at Polygon and continued his work on communication systems until December 1944. He also continued to work with SIME on other projects.

Chapter 24

Mentioned in Despatches and British Empire Medal

In 1943, Rowley was 'Mentioned in despatches' in notices which appeared in a supplement to the *London Gazette* dated Thursday 24th June 1943. With the approval of the King, the War Office published a list of personnel whom it wished to highlight for "gallant and distinguished services in the Middle East during the period 1st May 1942 to 22nd October 1942".

In early 1943 the 'A' Force Commander, Colonel Dudley Clarke, recommended Rowley for the British Empire Medal (BEM). In his commendation, Dudley Clarke made specific mention of the recent Allied Forces landings in North Africa.

The original Army form, W3121, which details the action for which Rowley was commended, was signed by Colonel Dudley W. Clarke and countersigned by Lt. General Ronald M. Scobie – Commander-in-Chief Middle East Forces. It was received by Army GHQ on 20th April 1943.

Action for which Commended (exact wording and spelling from form W3121):

"**This NCO has practiced a civilian hobby in peacetime in connection with wireless telegraphy which has given him almost unique qualifications for most highly secret work which is the direct concern of the organisation under my control. For a period of over eighteen months, he has worked for us voluntarily in his after-duty hours in addition to his normal work. For the past nine months this work has** occupied him nightly for two to three hours on at least six nights a week.

The work is entirely personal and would cease if Sjt. Shears could not continue it. During a period of illness when he was confined to bed and under medical care, this NCO insisted on going on a stretcher to his place of duty nightly and carrying on with the work. Its success over a long period, often under conditions of great difficulty, is due very largely to the high technical skill, keenness, perseverance and ingenuity of Sjt. SHEARS.

The results of this successful work have had a definite strategic effect upon all major MEF operations since November 1941, in addition to those involving the Allied forces' landings in N. AFRICA".

NB: Form W3121 information (as reproduced above) has been provided by The National Archives and contains public sector information licensed under the Open Government Licence v3.0

The award of the BEM (Military Division) was announced in the *London Gazette* on the 14th October 1943. It mentions that it is awarded in recognition of "gallant and distinguished services in the Middle East". In both the official notices, Rowley is referred to as a sergeant, his grade when he started worked with SIME. Formal recognition of his commission was not given until July 1943. Rowley sent a letter home to his parents in spring 1943 to tell them that his commission (to lieutenant) had finally come through as confirmed. This was reported in the local Barnet newspaper in August 1943 and subsequently appeared in the *London Gazette* on the 10th March 1944.

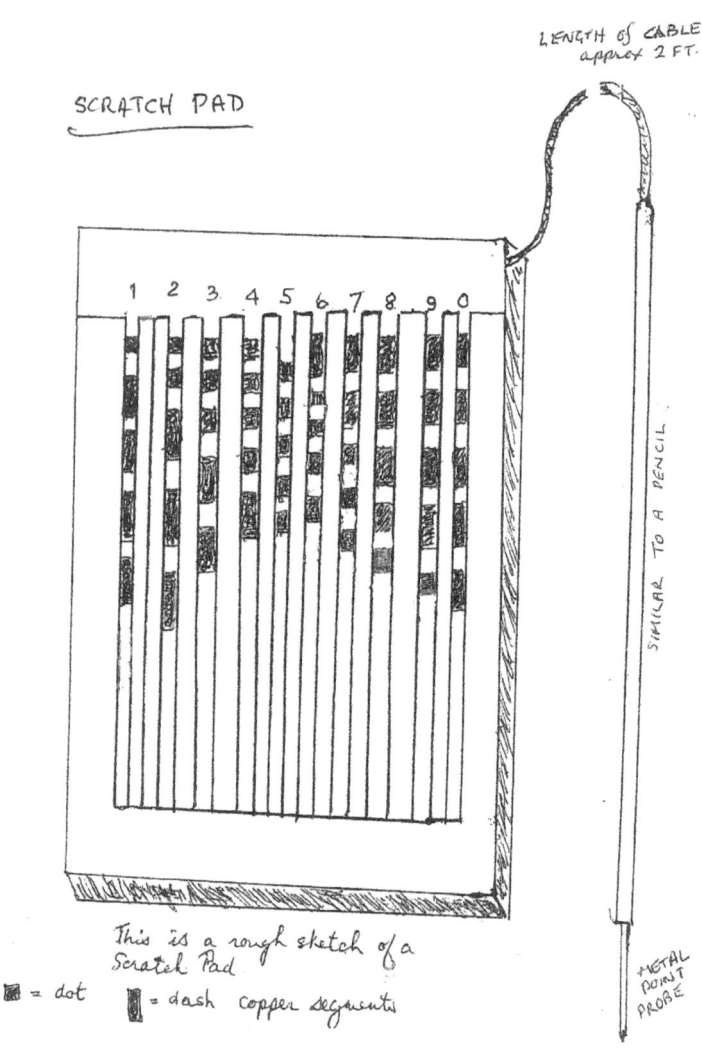

Scratch pad box sketch, by Rowley - used by agents for simple Morse transmissions

Name / Ὄνομα SPEARS, ROWLAND GEORGE RATCLIFF.	**SPECIAL PASS,**
Rank and Unit / Βαθμός καὶ μονάς 2/LIEUT. S.I.L.E.	**AUTHORITY & IDENTITY CARD.**
Height / Ἀνάστημα 5'7"	
Colour of Eyes / Χρῶμα ὀφθαλμῶν GREEN.	Date of Expiry 31 Dec 45
Colour of Hair / Χρῶμα κόμης	No.
Any person finding this card should take it at once to the nearest Allied Military Head-quarters, where he will be rewarded.	**ΕΙΔΙΚΟΝ ΔΕΛΤΙΟΝ**
Ὅπιος δήποτε εὕρῃ τὸ παρὸν δελτίον παρακαλεῖται ὅπως τὸ φέρῃ ἀμέσως εἰς τὸ πλησιέστερον Συμμαχικὸν Στρατηγεῖον καὶ ἀμοιφθήσεται.	**ΕΓΚΡΙΤΙΚΗ ΑΔΕΙΑ ΚΑΙ ΔΕΛΤΙΟΝ ΤΑΥΤΟΤΗΤΟΣ**
	Ἡμερομηνία λήξεως
	Ἀριθμὸς

The bearer of this Card is engaged on Special Duties. He is authorised to be in any place, in any dress, at any time, in the execution of his duty.

All persons subject to Military Law are enjoined to give him every assistance in their power and all others are requested to give him all facilities.

Ὁ κάτοχος τοῦ παρόντος δελτίου ἐκτελεῖ εἰδικὴν ὑπηρεσίαν. Πρὸς ἐκτέλεσιν τῆς ὑπηρεσίας του ταύτης δικαιοῦται νὰ εἰσέρχεται εἰς οἰονδήποτε μέρος καὶ νὰ φέρῃ οἰανδήποτε ἐνδυμασίαν ἐν οἰᾳδήποτε στιγμῇ.

Οἱ ὑποκείμενοι εἰς τὸν Στρατιωτικὸν νόμον ὅπως λάβῃ ὁδηγίας νὰ παρέχωσι εἰς αὐτὸν πᾶσαν δυνατὴν βοήθειαν, πάντες δὲ οἱ ἄλλοι καλοῦνται νὰ παρέχωσιν εἰς αὐτὸν πᾶσαν δυνατὴν εὐκολίαν.

Signed for, and on behalf of the Commander-in-Chief Allied Forces,
Headquarters Middle East.

Photo of bearer: / Φωτογραφία κατόχου:

Signature of bearer: / Ὑπογραφὴ κατόχου: R.R.Spears

Ὑπογράφεται ἀντὶ καὶ ἐν ὀνόματι τοῦ Ἀρχιστρατήγου τῶν Συμμαχικῶν Δυνάμεων.

Γενικὸν Στρατηγεῖον Μ. Α.

SIME issued Special 'Green' Pass for Greece

By the KING'S Order the name of
Sergeant R. G. Shears,
Royal Corps of Signals
was published in the London Gazette on
24 June, 1943,
as mentioned in a Despatch for distinguished service.
I am charged to record
His Majesty's high appreciation.

Secretary of State for War

Mentioned in a Despatch certificate, June 1943

BUCKINGHAM PALACE.

I greatly regret that I am
unable to give you personally the
award which you have so well earned.

I now send it to you with
my congratulations and my best
wishes for your future happiness.

George R.I.

Sergeant Rowland G. Shears,
BEM
12th. August, 1946.

British Empire Medal and letter from King George VI, August 1946

Chapter 25
1944 – Undercover in Crete (May) and Task Force to Athens (October)

In one of Rowley's CVs (written in 1978) he noted that in 1944 he was promoted to the rank of captain in intelligence and spent more time with SIME, and less on radio communications. It's clear from his written accounts that Rowley's Signals unit facilitated his SIME work and that during certain SIME operations he was fully utilised by them during his working hours. This is particularly apparent in Rowley's accounts of two secret operations which he undertook as part of the SIME and Force 133 (SOE) during 1944, firstly in Crete in the Eastern Mediterranean and then secondly in mainland Greece.

His formal army records for this time always recorded him as being in 3 Company 3GHQ Signals.

By 1944 Rowley was working with a unit called Force 133 which was part of SOE (Special Operations Executive) but run from Cairo, and whilst he was being asked by his Abwehr contacts for information about Allied activities in Greece, was already well aware of a number of successful actions carried out by this group using 'Caiques' (Greek-styled fishing sail boats) around the islands of the Ionian sea. Part of his awareness of these activities stemmed from his personal involvement in the successful operation to capture General Karl Kreipe, Commander of the German forces in Crete. The operation was led by Major Patrick Leigh-Fermor and his second in command Captain W. Stanley Moss (Billy). They had support from a small group of special forces and local Cretan partisans. Patrick Leigh-Fermor had spent some time in Crete before this event working with the partisans (Andartes), so was familiar with the terrain. He and his party captured the General whilst he was being chauffeured in his staff car on the evening of April 26th 1944.

Rowley's role in this plot required him to land on the island of Crete to provide radio net support between the "kidnapping group" and the Royal Navy who were providing the transportation to and from Crete. Rowley landed on Crete with a small group and met up with Major Leigh-Fermor and his group once they had succeeded in their kidnap plan. Rowley recounts being escorted by seven or eight well-armed Cretan partisans to a mountain cave where they all waited for Rowley to receive the 'all-clear' from the Royal Navy to proceed to the pick-up point. Radio conditions were poor for a while which delayed their leaving. The Royal Navy gave the 'all-clear' signal after several hours of complete darkness during which time the German spotter planes gave up their search and returned to their base. The final message from the Navy was that they were launching a long boat to come and pick them up at a sandy beach situated about 20-25 minutes away from the cave they were in. Rowley notes that he put all of his radio equipment back into his transit case and walked to the beach with the General and his British guards. He commented that the General took it all in good faith and seemed to accept his predicament. They were soon on the Royal Navy corvette and on their way back to Egypt.

As the British team were working 'under cover' on Crete and were not in their army uniforms they would have been executed had they been caught. Although the successful kidnap was a morale boost for the British, the German Army on Crete instigated severe reprisals against the local population for their support of it.

Later, in 1950, Captain Moss published a book *Ill Met by Moonlight*, which described the planning and execution of the operation. In 1957 a film of the same name, and starring Dirk Bogarde as Leigh-Fermor, was released. Rowley is not mentioned in the book but to show his appreciation of Rowley's support on the operation, 'Billy' Moss presented a personally signed copy to him.

In Autumn 1944, as the Germans started to retreat from Greece, Rowley (still in Cairo) received a message from the Abwehr indicating that they may have to withdraw from Athens. With this message, there was also an urgent request that he, as their agent in Cairo, should investigate the possibility of getting over to the Greek mainland, to continue working for them. They advised him to travel without any wireless equipment as they had plans to leave some in the Athens area for him to collect. A suggestion was also made that he could possibly get work as a civilian with a transport company. He was advised to renew his passport and that funds would be forthcoming.

Before replying to the message from the Abwehr, Rowley had several meetings to discuss how it would be possible for a German civilian to make his way from Cairo to Athens. The transportation arrangements needed to be as authentic as possible. After the meetings, SIME Movements section was asked to make enquiries about the re-establishment of non-military shipping services between Cairo and Piraeus, the sea port for Athens. Within a few days, the answer came that a Greek merchant vessel was being prepared for work on a Royal Navy contract to carry non-military supplies, such as food and medical items, between Cairo and Piraeus on a weekly basis. The first sailing was expected to take place in about two weeks once the approaches to Piraeus harbour and the harbour itself had been cleared of mines.

Rowley sent a reply to the Abwehr to advise that he had identified some Greek vessels in Egypt which were currently being worked on to make them seaworthy again. He advised them that once Piraeus harbour was clear of mines, following the withdrawal of German troops, he would be able to purchase a cabin on board one of the vessels for $2,000. Advising that he would make his own arrangements for passport and Greek travel permit, which was expected to cost a further $5,000, meant that he needed around $10,000 to support this mission.

Three days later a reply was received confirming that he should make the necessary plans for his travel and that $12,000 was being despatched, via courier, as before. He was also advised that instructions would soon be sent on how to make contact once he arrived in Athens.

One-week later Rowley and Kling were called to a meeting at GHQ (Grey Pillars) where they were instructed to proceed to Alexandria to join the task force (Central Mediterranean Forces) for the re-invasion of Greece. They were told that the force would include British, South African, Australian and Gurkhas as well as a Greek contingent and would number more than 10,000 men together with Royal Navy and RAF personnel and their task forces. Rowley and Kling were told to wear their uniforms of rank; to pack some civilian clothes and ensure they had their SIME 'Green Passes'.

Rowley got back to his radio workshop at Polygon with just 10 minutes to spare before his scheduled contact time with the Abwehr. He was advised that they had an unusually long message to send. Their messages normally took an average of five to six minutes to receive but this one took 27 minutes! The next day Rowley went to the Radio Centre at Gezira Island where he met Kling to discuss the content of the, now decoded, long message from the previous night. Kling's greeting to him on arrival included the question, "Have you got your bags packed?"

The long message confirmed that Rowley, their agent, should head to Athens immediately and should report to the officer in charge of a small town in an Athens suburb called Psychiko. He was advised that as he approached Psychiko on the main road from Athens he would find a large house with aerials in the garden. Rowley notes that British Intelligence already knew of this place. The message also confirmed that arrangements were being made to bury a transmitter/receiver along with instructions for operating including frequencies, call signs and details for encoding. Very precise and detailed instructions on where and how to locate the transmitter/receiver were also received and he was asked to memorise these. The equipment was to be buried in a forest on the outskirts of Psychiko, one metre underground by a large tree marked with a circle in white paint. It was suggested that he should locate it in daylight and then recover the equipment (approx. 20kg in weight) at night. After being reminded to take garden tools with him for this task he was wished "good luck".

This proved to be Rowley's last transmission with the Abwehr as things were moving very quickly. Rowley notes that Kling's greeting on his arrival on Gezira (about his bag being packed) meant that Kling had heard from Geoffrey West, another SIME officer, that they, plus a dozen or so SIME officers and NCOs, were now on standby to proceed to Greece by sea transport in a convoy escorted by Royal Navy vessels.

As Rowley was due to leave Cairo, his reserve operator, Anne, was called in to receive and transmit messages to/from the Abwehr. He notes that he later learnt that only one message was received during his time away in Greece, even though Anne had kept a 'listening watch'. This indicated that the Abwehr had started to move north from Athens well before he arrived there.

Rowley recounts that they arrived at the port in Alexandria amid lots of activity with tanks, artillery, ammunition and vehicles (most of them still wearing their 'desert camouflage' colouring), being loaded onto to various vessels. There were troop carriers, several frigates, destroyers, minesweepers and the largest, a liner, the Canadian-Pacific *Princess Kathleen*. The SIME contingent boarded the *Princess Kathleen*. Before leaving port, they were allocated cabins 'down below' but Kling, Rowley and a few others opted to sleep on deck rather than in the allocated cabins as they were so hot with very little ventilation. The Captain addressed all troops over the 'Tannoy' system to announce a safety drill before they sailed and reminded everybody that they should not smoke on deck after the hours of darkness. He addressed everyone again after the safety drill and informed them of the route they would be taking to Piraeus, approximately 700 miles from Alexandria. He explained that, under

Royal Navy protection, they would set sail on a safer route far to the east of Crete (which was still occupied by the Germans) to be there during the early morning hours of darkness, and then arrive in Piraeus around midday, the day after tomorrow.

Once the convoy had passed the Crete danger zone, most of the Royal Navy vessels went on ahead to Piraeus to check out the coastal defences and look for any mines in Piraeus harbour. On learning that the Germans had heavily mined the approaches to the harbour, the captain of the liner was told to anchor two miles outside the harbour at Piraeus. From that viewpoint, those on board watched the Royal Navy minesweepers doing their work on clearing those mines.

The SIME group were amongst the first to disembark from 'the Princess', on the 12th October 1944, along with about 60 other officers and men from the Royal Engineers. They all boarded the diesel-engine-powered light landing crafts, each with its own skipper, and began to make their way towards the jetties within the harbour. As they made their way forward, Rowley was aware of a tank landing craft about 30 yards away from them on the starboard side. There was a sudden tremendous noise as that craft struck a mine and exploded. There were casualties on the tank landing craft but none on Rowley's craft. However, the explosion did cause him to lose some hearing in his left ear, which also was further damaged in 1983 when he happened to be at Harrods department store, in London, when a bomb went off.

Once ashore, the SIME group collected their Jeeps and with four of them in each vehicle, made their way inland to the capital, Athens. They had been advised that the Germans were still withdrawing from the Athens area and an Infantry reconnaissance patrol had confirmed that the main road from Piraeus to Athens had been checked for mines and there was no sign of any resistance. Rowley noted that they didn't see any sign of Luftwaffe aircraft on the route but proceeded slowly to the centre of Athens where they had been advised to report to the office of the Commander-in-Chief, situated at the King George V hotel (now known as King George hotel). Once they had driven out of the port area, they had no choice but to drive slowly as the Athenian welcome was tremendous. Rowley remarks that he would always remember the welcome as all the streets were decked in flowers, with lots being thrown into the Jeeps. There were kisses from the girls and slaps on the back from the men and boys.

On arrival at the hotel, they found the hotel reception to be full of British officers trying to check in for a few nights. Space was very limited and only senior officers were allocated rooms. Rowley's group were given two rooms for three nights. Rowley recalls that he and Kling, being the smallest in their party, volunteered to sleep in a bath, within a private bathroom, on alternate nights. This resulted in very uncomfortable nights and in his notes, he comments that it was lucky that the toilet was in a separate room!

Geoffrey West, Rowley's SIME colleague, had made contact with his 'underground' man in Athens, named Konstantinidis (code name 'Albert'). Albert, his brave family and a wider network had arranged for Brits, Australians and New Zealanders to be repatriated to Egypt after they were left behind in Greece earlier in the war when the German army drove from south-east Europe and into Greece. They had also repatriated Allied air crews who were shot down over Greece when on bombing raids from Egypt.

Konstantinidis agreed to find out whether any German troops were still in the Psychiko area. Ninety minutes later he returned, having sent one of his daughters there via the longer route, using lanes and fields. She went into Psychiko and everywhere there were signs of a German withdrawal, with vehicles loaded and tanks being refuelled from jerry cans. She thought at one point she was being followed but managed to slip away from the soldier in German uniform by disappearing into the dense forest land before making her way back home. Geoffrey thanked him and his son and four daughters. He also sent sincere regrets to the family about the loss of their mother, Madame Konstantinidis, who had been shot by a

German SS firing squad the day before Rowley arrived in Piraeus. She and her two eldest daughters had been in prison and tortured as suspect leaders of the underground network, but they never disclosed any information. Rowley comments that he was later shown the field and the exact point where this murder had taken place and there were masses of flowers still there. He was honoured to attend a very moving ceremony at the re-established British Embassy when the family Konstantinidis was awarded the 'Order of the British Empire', presented by the new British Ambassador on orders from Winston Churchill.

After receiving the update on German troop movements around the Psychiko area, Rowley and his team had a meeting with Geoffrey and other SIME officers to discuss their mission to locate the Abwehr radio station and operational Headquarters near Psychiko and, if possible, capture the Abwehr staff. They received the latest intelligence reports just before sunrise and were told about the German Army retreat northwards which was taking place all through the night in the Athens area and suburbs.

They had been shown a helpful map, drawn up by Albert, which showed the location of the villa in Psychiko, occupied by Abwehr staff for their operational activities. It showed that the property, surrounded by a garden full of aerial masts, was about 200 metres from the Psychiko end of the main road which started in central Athens, almost in front of the George V hotel. The villa was called 'Ariadne in the Setting Sun'. The front entrance was on a service road, and there was a grass strip, about 50 metres wide, bordering the main road. To the right of the property was a small suburban road leading to other properties. The main entrance was on the left of the building and about 50 metres from the entrance gate. With this information, the team decided to split into two groups of equal numbers: a total of twelve men including two drivers for the Jeeps. One group would be led by Captain Kling and the other by Rowley. Accompanied by their fully armed staff sergeants, Kling and Rowley carried their own .38 pistols.

Parking the vehicles about 300 metres from the entrance to the grounds, they then surrounded the villa and after surveying it for a while from amongst the rows of laterally planted fruit trees (and plenty of blackcurrant bushes) to the rear of the property, they entered it.

The Germans had already fled, but obviously in a hurry as they had left equipment and secret coding books behind. They had no luck in finding the buried radio equipment as previously described by Rowley's Abwehr contact before he left Cairo.

After the Germans had left Athens and the British arrived to take control, there was a great amount of instability. During the time Rowley was in Greece the situation in Athens was very volatile and often dangerous. Rowley used to recount that on some days when he was out in his Jeep it was beneficial for the Athenians to believe he was American rather than British. The soft felt-styled officers' cap he had purchased whilst in Cairo, which was similar to those worn by the Americans, proved to be a very useful piece of kit on those days!

Rowley left Greece on the 23rd December 1944 and went back to Cairo. His time with SIME and 'A' Force had now concluded and he was transferred back to the Signals. He was repatriated to the UK towards the end of January 1945 and arrived back at Glasgow on 21st February 1945. After his long service overseas, he was now due some extended leave in the UK under the Python scheme, which ensured that those who had completed service overseas for over four years were prioritised to come back to the UK. Once back in the UK, Rowley had been instructed to "report in writing" to the London District Reception Depot at Duke of Yorks Headquarters, Chelsea SW3, to confirm his home address.

In recognition of his war service, Rowley received a number of medals at the end of the war in addition to the British Empire Medal which he had been awarded in 1943.

He was awarded the Royal Signals Territorial Decoration (TD), which was announced in the *London Gazette* on the 3rd October

1947. In 1948, he received the Defence Medal (1939–45) plus a War Medal with a single oak leaf clasp, as he had been mentioned in despatches. He also received three specific campaign (star) medals for war service. These were: the 1939–1945 Star, the Italy Star (for service in Sicily, Italy as well as the Aegean and Greece) and the Africa Star.

In 1946, Rowley received his British Empire medal along with a letter signed by King George VI, which expressed his regret that he had not been able to present it to him personally.

Part III
POST WAR GERMANY

Chapter 26
Military Life Continues in 1945

With the war now over, Rowley, like many others of his generation, had to consider his future – either a return to civilian life in the UK or further time with the military.

Before he left Cairo, he had approached his commanding officer in the Signals, Lieutenant Colonel E Nepean, with a written formal request that his commission on the General List be transferred to the Royal Corps of Signals before he was to be repatriated to the UK. This letter was the first in a protracted round of communications on this issue by Rowley and his Signals Officer, Major Charles Kidd, to the officials at the Royal Signals and the War Office, trying to persuade them to confirm this transfer. Because he had been commissioned in the field and had not attended a full officer training course (OCTU), the Signals were reluctant to accept him as an officer. Rowley was instructed to attend a six-month OCTU course in Catterick in April 1945. Meanwhile, Rowley's expertise was required at the Control Commission for Germany and Major Kidd, who was now working with the Commission, continued to write to the War Office and Signals to try to expedite his transfer. The Control Commission was working to restore the local government and administration arrangements for the British zone and consisted of both military and civil servant personnel. Germany had no central government or administration anymore and each of the occupied zones, American, British, French and Russian, were being managed separately.

In April 1945, Rowley, as instructed, presented himself at the School of Signals, Catterick Camp, for the required instruction. Almost immediately, the Commander of Catterick sent a letter to the Royal Signals and the War office, copied to Central Control

Commission, to say that in view of Rowley's previous experience and the work he was about to take on "there is comparatively little I can teach him here which would be of any use to him". It was settled that he would attend a post 'Python leave' refresher course instead. Whilst at Catterick, he assisted with the training of others and finally, at the end of April 1945, he received confirmation that his transfer to the Royal Signals as an officer had been accepted with effect from 20th April 1945.

Rowley was posted to the Royal Signals depot at Thirsk, Yorkshire at his existing rank and the appointment was published in the *London Gazette* on the 12th June 1945.

After the required training, Rowley was transferred to 1 War Office Signals at Droitwich, Worcester on 30th June 1945 which utilised his services until Central Control Commission in Germany were able to complete the appropriate paperwork for his transfer there. Whilst stationed there, he applied to the British GPO (General Post Office), for his amateur radio licence to be reissued under his original call sign of G8KW.

Chapter 27
1945: Journey to Germany – The Long Arm of Coincidence

Rowley finally arrived in Germany in August 1945 and joined the Radio Section of the Posts and Telecommunications Branch of the Control Commission. He was promoted to the rank of acting Captain, Royal Signals, within the British Army of the Rhine (BAOR).

Rowley's account of his journey to Germany, and the first jobs he undertook, is detailed in this chapter.

Rowley recalled that in early 1939 he imported from 'The Rothermel Brush Company, USA', three of their famous D104 crystal microphones. One for himself, and two for his licensed amateur friends, Reg Pidsley, G6PI from Potters Bar, and John Clarricoats, G6CL. Together they cost the sum of £9, including postage and customs duty.

After his posting to Germany was confirmed in June 1945, Rowley reported to 'Officers Movements' in London and was issued with transit tickets and told to report the following morning at Croydon Airport for an RAF flight to Brussels. This airport still lacked a proper runway and, as it had been raining for the past two days on the grass field, it was not possible for a Dakota plane to take off. After reporting back on the two following days and there being no improvement to the weather conditions, Rowley went back to 'Movements' to see if there was an alternative routing available. There, he met a helpful captain and he explained to him that he needed to get to RAF Bückeburg, in Germany. The captain offered an underground rail ticket to Fenchurch Street from where he could take a steam train to Tilbury Docks in Essex. Rowley was told that there were some tank landing crafts going across to Antwerp and from there he should find plenty of army trucks going to Brussels. The captain issued a signed pass to allow Rowley to hitch a ride to Brussels. Once there, he was told to locate RAF 'Movements' and they should find him a Dakota going from Brussels airport to RAF Bückeburg.

Rowley recalls that the North Sea crossing was not good as it was slow and the movement of the craft resembled a large swing ride at a funfair. On arrival at Antwerp docks, late on a Saturday evening, he was offered food and accommodation for the night in the Officers' Transit Mess. Whilst there, he enquired about any transport or the possibility of a lift to Brussels. The Mess Sergeant informed him that there was only one road out of Antwerp, which met the main road to Brussels, due to all the bridges having been destroyed. It was suggested that Rowley should try to hitch a lift by waiting at the roadside at the east end of that bridge, and the Sergeant offered to drop him there at nine o'clock the next morning.

The traffic was light on a Sunday morning as Rowley waited by the bridge, and a few tanks went by, two despatch riders on motorcycles and several RAF heavy lorries. Eventually a Jeep came over the bridge with a rigid van-like rear section. As it got closer, there were large letters on the front spelling 'BBC'. The driver stopped and Rowley immediately recognised the front passenger as Reg Pidsley, whom he had not seen, or heard of, since 1939. Once they had recovered from seeing each other, Reg introduced him to the well-known news reporter that he was travelling with. Reg told Rowley that he was a BBC recording engineer with the BBC War Reporting Unit and that his D104 microphone was still going strong, and it was sometimes used with his present recording equipment. He removed the microphone from its velvet sleeve, and it still looked like new! Rowley recounts that they talked all the way to Brussels until Reg deposited him at Movements Control.

One of Reg's wartime jobs had been to accompany a reporter, Wynford Vaughan-Thomas, on a night-time raid over Berlin on 3rd September 1943 to capture recordings of the action and voices of the crew to commemorate the fourth anniversary of Britain entering the war. Accounts of this trip and the famous recording can still be found and heard, online, today.

The following day Rowley was on a Dakota and finally on his way to RAF Bückeburg from where he reported to the CO at the Signals Unit on the Army base at Bad Oeynhausen, a spa town in North Rhine-Westphalia. This area became the Headquarters for the British Army of the Rhine (BAOR) as well as that of the British sector, Central Control Commission for Germany.

Chapter 28

Back to Broadcasting at Langenberg, Germany

Now in Germany, Rowley notes that his first job with the Control Commission for Germany was as officer in charge of rebuilding the Broadcast Station for Radio Cologne, at Langenberg in the Rhineland, following its destruction in April 1945. It was important that the public broadcasting network was revived as soon as possible so that a reliable means of communications with the population could be established. Whilst in Langenberg, Rowley stayed at 'Hordthaus' guesthouse, which was quite near the radio station, and he had the use of a German-made Wanderer car (part of Auto Union manufacturing group).

Rowley recounts that two 100 kW medium-wave transmitters at Langenberg, built by Telefunken and Siemens, had been blown up by the German SS in April 1945 when General Patten's US troops were approaching the area. Other equipment at the site, including the cooling equipment, had been blown up in the cellar below the main transmitters hall, the oil-filled capacitors and transformers had been bayoneted, and hand grenades had been thrown onto the 6ft high power amplifier (PA) stages. The 200-metre-tall radio mast, one of the highest in Europe at the time, had also been felled. A picture of the original (pre-1945) masts is shown in the pictures section.

As officer in charge, Rowley ordered some new masts from Bochum (Rhineland). Working with a team of three sergeants, (plus a cook) and three of the ex-station staff, it took around three months to completely rebuild the station and get it fully back on the air, although Rowley noted that they managed the first transmission to the Ruhr area in September, having erected two new 260 ft (80metre) masts in August 1945. Fortunately, the SS had overlooked the modulator transformer which was still intact, and Rowley's team managed to get one transmitter working with a temporary triangular aerial system. This enabled them to commence transmissions for the 'Nordwestdeutscher Rundfunk' (North West German broadcasting) and Rowley notes that what they installed continued to work for a further fifteen years into the early 1960s as he sometimes listened to the station when he was back home in the UK.

Rowley had managed to trace the former radio station manager, Arthur Wurbs, who was at a prisoner of war camp in Holland, and arranged an early release for him so that he could resume his former role. Wurbs, whom Rowley had known as a fellow radio ham before the outbreak of war, had been 50 when he was called up into the German Signals Corps, in the closing months of the war. It was useful for Rowley to have some of the old staff back and Wurbs was very pleased that Rowley had helped him. Rowley recalls how Wurbs described the pre-war meetings he had attended to agree the original siting of the station in Langenberg, and this location eventually being chosen for its elevation and the ability to transmit to the Ruhr area as well as Düsseldorf and Cologne.

Whilst in this role, Rowley was confirmed to a full captaincy in November 1945. His work on the radio station set-up lasted until February 1946.

Rowley didn't document his memoirs in great detail after this point. The information in the following chapters of the rest of the book, covering his life post-1945, has been gleaned from some specific postwar stories which Rowley mentioned in his memoir introduction, a variety of letters and notes, notes on photographs and formal documents, as well as my (the author's) personal family knowledge/recollections.

Chapter 29
Police Radio Network – Hamburg, Germany (1946–1947)

From mid-January 1946 Rowley moved to Hamburg and initially lived at 93B Elbe Chaussee. His role in the Radio & Research section of the Control Commission for Germany (Radio Section, P & T Branch, Hamburg) was initially as the deputy assistant controller and he was made assistant controller from 1st July 1946. One of his key tasks was to take charge of reactivating the German Police Radio network throughout the British controlled zone of Germany. Over the next few years, he organised the upgrade and roll-out of radio systems, operating on ultra-high frequency wavebands, to all the key cities in the British zone and this was still operating well when he left Germany in 1950.

Rowley was granted the rank of acting major on the 6th September 1946 and achieved the distinction of being the youngest major in the Royal Corps of Signals at just twenty-seven years plus two days of age. This event was published in the *London Gazette* on 3rd October 1947. He was confirmed as a full major on 6th December 1946.

Whilst based in Hamburg, Rowley recalled travelling by steam traction engine on cobbled roads to get to the Officers' Country Club in Hamburg on Boxing Day 1946. On the back of a grainy picture of the traction engine (in the pictures section) he noted that he was accompanied by Charles Kidd and another colleague called 'Dickie'.

At the end of 1946, changes to military strength in Germany were being organised and Rowley was informed that he was eligible to obtain Class A release from the Army. In September 1946, he received an offer of employment from the 'Control Office for Germany & Austria' to transfer to the Control Commission for Germany in his existing role at a salary of £640 per annum so he wrote to Lieutenant Colonel Charles Kidd to request his release from the Signals.

Rowley was struck off Signals unit strength on the 16th January 1947, and during his 130 days leave from 17th January 1947 until 26th May 1947 he headed home to see his family. He was released from Army service (demobilised) on the 27th May 1947 and now as a civilian, continued to do the same work as before with his former military colleagues.

Chapter 30
The Control Commission for Germany

From 1947, Rowley continued his work for the Control Commission for Germany and for the next few years he worked in Hamburg, Berlin or Frankfurt. He noted that he was also involved in some intelligence work during this time.

The Control Office (for Germany and Austria) ceased to be an independent unit in April 1947, when it was incorporated into the British Foreign Office. The Control Commission for Germany was then under the management of the Foreign Office until it ended in 1949 when Germany was officially declared a republic.

In 1947 Rowley was the British delegate of the Radio Working Party Quadripartite Committee in Berlin, along with representatives of the American, Russian and French authorities in Germany. He attended international radio/communication conferences in Geneva, The Hague and Copenhagen as the delegate for the British zone in Germany. He was also secretary of the British Signal Communications Board.

In 1948, Rowley was the Chief Signals Officer, Berlin, and was responsible for all radio communications during the Russian blockade and the Berlin airlift, when food and other supplies were delivered into Berlin by aircraft. The Soviet military administration shut down traffic by rail, canal, and road into and out of West Berlin in June 1948 and those restrictions weren't lifted until May 1949. Rowley arrived in Berlin in early 1948 and at some stage went back to Hamburg before returning to Berlin briefly in 1949.

In 1949, Rowley was attached to the Bipartite (British and American administrations working together) Control Office (Communications Section) in Frankfurt. He was the British Member of the Bi-partite Signals board in Frankfurt and, in March 1949, was part of a team of experts put together to study the establishment of a radio service for ships navigating the Rhine. Rowley represented the British military government in Germany and attended the meetings in The Hague in March 1949. The conference put forward proposals for River Rhine radio communications and Rowley went on a River Rhine test trip on May 17th 1949.

Chapter 31
The First Train into Berlin at the End of the Russian Blockade (May 12th 1949)

When the blockade was eventually lifted, Rowley was asked by his colonel to get from Hamburg to Helmstedt (in the Allied zone but close to the Russian controlled border), to be on the first train, leaving at midnight, for Berlin. Rowley was to provide communications links for newspaper reporters who were sent to report on whether the train service would run uninterrupted into Berlin and not be stopped at any stage by the Russian military. He received his orders by phone at 13.00 hours and was told to take his transmitter/receiver 'B2 TX/RX' (also known as a 'Type 3 Mk II' and sometimes called a B2-spyset). A picture of one is shown in the photos section. The colonel said he would arrange frequencies, accumulators, wire for the aerial (to cover the length of a carriage) and call signs and would also arrange for a coastal radio station, on the German North Sea, to keep a signal watch. In order to send messages, Rowley initially rigged up an aerial system on the outside of the train carriage and set up his radio equipment during the journey. Rowley notes that General Sir Brian Robertson and his intelligence advisers were afraid the train would be stopped on the way during the seven-hour journey. Fortunately, it wasn't and Rowley was kept busy all night sending messages, in Morse, for 40 newspaper reporters who wished to broadcast news of this event to their worldwide audiences. These messages were passed on by the operator at Cuxhaven Radio on the North Sea coast.

Captain Rowland George Shears, 1945

Radio Langenberg masts before being destroyed

Radio Langenberg mast under construction, 1945

Radio Langenberg new mast in Winter 1946

Rowley with his 'Wanderer' car at Langenberg

Rowley's D2KW / G8KW QSL card

Traction Engine transport on Boxing Day, Hamburg, 1946

OFFICE OF THE ~~THEATER~~ CHIEF SIGNAL ~~OFFICER~~ DIVISION
EUROPEAN ~~THEATER~~ COMMAND
APO 757 US ARMY

AMATEUR RADIO STATION AND OPERATOR'S LICENSE

Under the provisions of Signal Standing Operating Procedure No. 56 and Signal Operation Instructions No. 22-1 HQs U. S. Forces European Theater, and upon evidence of conformity with the licensing provisions of Secs. 002.01, 003.01 & 004.05 of S. O. I. No. 22-1, this combined Amateur Operator's and Amateur Radio Station License is issued to:

R. G. Shears, British Civilian.
Bipartite Control Office, Communications Group,
425 HQ CCG, Frankfurt/Main, B.A.O.R. 21.
Yellow House, Falkenstein, Germany.

for a period of one (1) year from the date of issuance, unless sooner terminated or suspended by the Theater Chief Signal Officer.

Date of issuance: 17 December 1948.

For the THEATER CHIEF SIGNAL OFFICER
G. W. McCartin Capt.Sig.C.
issuing officer

CALL	SIGN
D4 A K W.	

AGPD-2024-11-45-1 T 32781

Rowley's D4AKW American Sector Licence, 1948

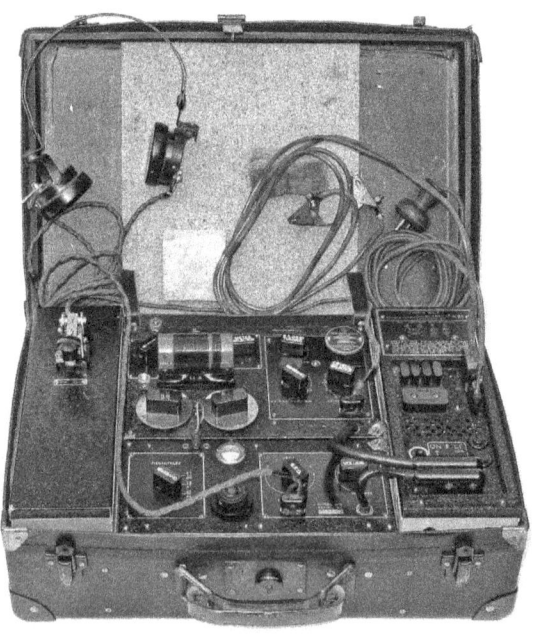

Type 3 Mk II spy radio set, (B2 spyset) in small suitcase (transmitter, receiver and power unit with headphones and Morse key)

Top: Group of seven District Managers for German radio ham groups in the British Zone
Bottom: Rowley (Major Shears), Lt.Col. Kidd and WJ Chalk
Both pictures taken after radio club (DARC) proposal meeting in Hamburg, May 1947

TELEPHONE HAMBURG 34 36 70 34 40 48 34 19 41 5	**RADIO SECTION** POSTS AND TELECOMMUNICATIONS BRANCH ~~HAMBURG DIVISION~~ CONTROL COMMISSION FOR GERMANY (BRITISH ELEMENT)	TELEGRAPHIC ADDRESS "RADMAR"

SUBJECT: **Formation of Amateur Radio Clubs for Short Wave Listening**

ZONAL EXECUTIVE OFFICES HAMBURG
63 HQ. C.C.G. B.A.O.R.

FILE REF. T6/63830/3/RGS

DATE: 19th June 1947

TO: Deutscher Amateur Radio Club,
(Britische Zone),
Geschäftsstelle Köln-Aachen,
Walter Führ, Wörthstr. 8,
K Ö L N

Geschäftsstelle Ruhr,
Hermann Ferring, Alstaderstr.77,
Oberhausen /Rhld.

Geschäftsstelle Berlin Britischer Sektor,
Rudi Hammer, Fuchsienweg 51,
Berlin - Rudow

1. Authority is hereby granted for the formation of the above named Club in the British Zone.

2. The conditions are as follows:-

   (a) All clubs are liable to be dissolved at the discretion of the local Military Government.

   (b) All groups of clubs must be controlled by a headquarters in the British Zone.

   (c) The names and addresses of all Presidents, Secretaries, and other holders of offices must be submitted to this office on July 15th 1947 and amended as changes occur. Lists of members will also be submitted on the same date and amended on the 15th of each month.

   (d) The Secretaries must be prepared to furnish any other information relative to the club's activities on request from this office.

   (e) Club or individual activities must not at present include work with transmitters or with any transmitting equipment

(R.G.SHEARS) Major.
for Controller.
Radio & Research Section.

IA

Copy to:
Herrn Müller, Kiel-Holtenau, Kanalstr.43.
ROOM 239
Reichspostdirektion
Stephansplatz
Hamburg 36

Control Commission (British) Authority letter for the formation of DARC

DEUTSCHER AMATEUR RADIO CLUB · BRITISCHE ZONE
(DARC/BZ)

Präsident: R. Rapcke, Hamburg 21, Uhlenhorster Weg 37 III
Vice Präsident: O. Lühra, Göttingen, Münchhausenstr. 14
Geschäftsführer: A. Müller, Kiel-Ellerbek, Kicelerstr. 113

To
Mr. R.G. Shears,
Frankfurt Office of the Controller General,
Post & Telecommunications (British)
Frankfurt/Main, B.A.O.R. 21

Ihr Zeichen	Ihre Nachricht vom	Unser Zeichen	Tag
		R/H	19.1.1950

Dear Mr. Shears,

        I very much regret that you have to leave us dear om Shears, as we know you have always been an active friend of the German Amateur Radio.

        I remember many occasions you advised and helped us, as a real amateur, in founding our clubs and in trying to obtain a transmitting licence. It has always been a great pleasure to know that with all difficulties we could apply to a friend who helped us whenever he could. You understood to get a special place in the hearts of German amateurs, and we shall always remember you with gratitude.

        I myself know from my own experience how much work and exact knowledge of getting the authorities to work in this special case was often necessary to make possible to obtain the transmitting licence. I also know it was you who convinced the gentlemen of the American Military Goverment that the German amateur was worthy to get a free working on the air. With this you did us an inestimable favour and therefore I beg you to except the "Honorary Membership" of the DARC/BZ.

        We should be extremely pleased if you excepted this, and you would be the "Honorary Member No. 1" and for the future the example that worldwide amateur radio is helping oneanother by international friendship. The amateurs are a big family all over the world and they know only one thing, that is: friendship and help, technical progress, and the ideas of our amateur sport.

        Further we are very much obliged to you for the recommendation to your colleagues of the Radio Section at Wahn. We sincerely hope to work with them in a good manner, and I thank you for your further help.

        Please do let me know as soon as possible whether we shall find you again under your old English call "G8KW" in your country, or on which place of the world we shall find you in the future. At any rate we shall note every new call with the suffix "KW".

        I close with my best wishes for your future and hope that we shall meet on the air many times.

Letter from DARC President, R.Rapcke, offering Honary Membership (No.1) to Rowley, 1950

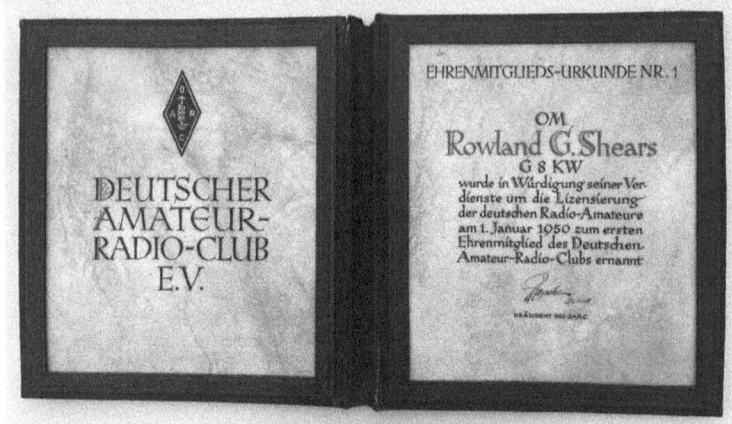

Honary Member No.1 - DARC Certificate

Junkers DRP (German made) Morse key - Rowley's favouite key

Chapter 32
Final Days in Frankfurt, Germany

During 1948, Rowley was based in Frankfurt and it is here that he met his future wife (my mother), Ruth. Ruth was also serving with the British Control Service in the Control Commission for Germany and was based in the headquarters of the Allied Military Command which itself was located in the former headquarters building of the chemical company, IG Farben. Ruth had been working there since June 1946, first as a teleprinter operator and later as a shorthand typist.

On the 1st January 1949, Rowley was appointed to the Regular Army Reserve of Officers (RARO) as a captain in the Royal Corps of Signals and was granted the honorary rank of major. An entry in the *London Gazette* appeared on 14th June 1949 to confirm this. He was retained on the RARO until 1974 when he reached the upper age limit allowed for reserve officers (55 years of age).

Due to a reduction in strength of the Commission, Rowley was advised by letter on 17th November 1949, that as of the 1st April 1950 his service with the Frankfurt office of the Controller General (Foreign Office), would be terminated.

Chapter 33
Working with the German Radio Amateurs (1946–1950)

Wishing to resume his amateur radio transmissions in Germany, Rowley had applied to the Secretary of the British Signal Communication Board (Amateur Radio – British zone) to be licensed for amateur transmissions. He had been issued with his own German call sign (D2KW) on 12th February 1946. At the time this arrangement was only available to operators in the British military. Later in 1948, whilst he was based in Frankfurt, he was also issued with call sign D4AKW by the American military for use in their zone. This licence is pictured in the photos section of this book.

In August 1946, whilst working on the police radio systems, and occasionally working with British intelligence, Rowley also took on the role of 'Organising Secretary' for British amateur radio activities in the British zone. Rowley obtained permission from Military HQ and the Director of Post and Communications of the British zone to organise and issue transmitting licences to members of the forces and civilians (British, Belgian, Dutch, Danish, Norwegian and Polish) who held licences pre-war or who had the necessary qualifications or trade ratings.

During 1946, amateur radio users in the UK, whose equipment had been taken away and whose transmitting licences had been withdrawn, were now starting to receive their impounded equipment and were reapplying for their licences. The radio amateurs were getting together to form radio clubs. Some bandwidths were still being used by the military at this time so there were some limitations on use. In Germany, at the same time, German amateurs were trying to get back on the airwaves too and although transmitting with radio waves was still illegal for the German population, many amateurs found a way to transmit. Some German amateurs visited Rowley whilst he was in Hamburg to enlist his help in getting things legalised.

In the British zone, radio amateur members of the Radio and Research Section of the Control Commission for Germany, led by Lieutenant Colonel Kidd (D2CK), were also keen to support the German amateurs with their aim of legal (registered/licensed) transmission and worked with Rowley in his role as organising secretary of the 'D2' amateurs, in order to achieve this. Because of the number of illegal transmissions, it seemed sensible to find a way to legalise the amateur operators who weren't engaging in black market activity or espionage.

On 17th May 1947, the district managers representing the seven different districts for radio hams in the British zone, met with Lieutenant Colonel Kidd, W.J. Chalk and Rowley from Posts & Telecommunications branch, in 'The Old Postal Building', Stephansplatz in Hamburg to go through the radio club proposals they had developed and put forward. Lieutenant Colonel Kidd gave verbal permission for the formation of DARC – Deutscher Amateur Radio Club (Britische Zone) and followed this up with a letter of formal authority, written in the German language, on 21st May 1947. The new club name had been proposed by the German radio hams who did not like the idea of carrying on with the old name of Deutscher Amateur Sende Dienst (DASD). At the time of set up, the club activities were not allowed to include "work with transmitters or any other transmitting equipment". Pictures from this time are shown in the photos section of this book.

On 19th June 1947 Rowley, on behalf of the controller in the Radio and Research section (Control Commission Germany), signed and issued an English translation of the formal permission letter for the formation of DARC.

Rowley continued to support the German radio hams in setting up their club and in their quest for official licences. He was helped with this task by General Brian Robertson who was Military Governor and C-in-C British Forces in Germany from October 1947. Rowley describes how he was in Berlin and was fixing up a radio circuit between Berlin and British HQ in Hamburg during the Russian blockade (from June 1948 to May 1949). Whilst fixing the radio telephone in General Robertson's office, the General walked in and Rowley remarks that "they had a long chat". From his 'intelligence' work Rowley was aware that it was very difficult to monitor the multitude of radio transmissions originating from Germany because the Allied interceptors, on the short-wave bands, did not know whether these messages were from agents (transmitting to the east and to Russia), enthusiastic radio amateurs or black marketeers. The outcome of the long chat with General Robertson was that he agreed that licences should be arranged for all German radio amateurs who had the appropriate credentials, so that the communications/signals from this group could easily be eliminated from the other two categories.

Robertson agreed to help by contacting his US and French opposite numbers and instructed Rowley to return to see him the next week. When Rowley did return, he was told that London had agreed at the highest level, the Americans were also on board and that he should now go ahead to arrange the licensing. Rowley notes that Robertson told him "Now go and organise it, Shears" and that the French took another six months to give their agreement.

Rowley did all he could to support this initiative. Registration and examinations for the amateurs were arranged from 1948. Full licensing didn't happen until 1949.

Approvals followed in the American zone and later in the French zone. All amateur radio call prefixes for Germany were standardised as DL. For German civilians DL1, DL3, DL6 and DL7 were allocated. Amateurs working for the organisations running the British, American and French zones were allocated DL2, DL4 and DL5 respectively. Thus, after these changes, Rowley's callsigns were updated from D2KW to DL2KW and from D4AKW to DL4KW (American zone).

At a meeting in Frankfurt in January 1948, it was decided to combine all of the individual radio associations of the Bizone (American and British occupation zones) into the German Amateur Radio Club (D.A.R.C.).

Later in 1948, Rowley and his colleagues were alerted to the fact that the Russian state was collecting any information they could about the radio hams operating in the West. In September of that year, Rowley, in his role as organising secretary for amateur radio in the British zone, and based in Berlin, sent a letter to all amateurs in the zone warning them about sending their QSL cards (and all the information contained on them) to the Soviet authorities (via Box 88 Moscow) when they wished to communicate with Russian amateurs. He advised that it was likely that Box 88 QSL Bureau was also operating as a recording centre for all the details submitted on the QSL cards.

Rowley continued to issue radio amateur licences until 1950 when he returned to the UK.

Rowley kept in touch with several of the founding members of Deutscher Amateur Radio Club (DARC) and they recognised him for his help during their set-up time, by making him the first honorary member of their club in January 1950. He received the letter confirming the award before he left Hamburg in early 1950 and was presented with an impressive official certificate, which had been hand crafted by a member of the radio club (Klein, DL1PS), in 1952. A picture of it is shown in the photos section.

The translation, from German, of the wording on the certificate says:

Honorary Member – Certificate No. 1
OM
Rowland G. Shears
G8KW

was appointed the first honorary member of the German Amateur Radio Club on January 1, 1950 in recognition of his services to the licensing of the German radio amateurs

(Signed):　　　　　　R. Rapcke
　　　　　　　　　　　DL1WA
　　　　　　　　　　　President DARC

Part IV
BACK IN THE UK and THE KW STORY

Chapter 34
Working in the UK

Rowley left the Control Commission, and Germany, at the beginning of 1950 and returned to the UK driving his silver 1950 Standard Vanguard Mark 1 saloon which he had purchased whilst in Germany.

Ruth and Rowley were married in Shirehampton, Bristol, in February 1950. Initially they settled in Welling, Kent, but later found a house at Birchwood Road, Wilmington, Kent which had a very long garden with enough room to accommodate Rowley's radio shacks, test equipment and aerials. A picture of the house is shown in the photos section.

Rowley considered working overseas again and gave some thought to a post with the Crown Agents for the Colonies but in the end stayed in the UK.

His first employment back in the UK was with Burndept Limited in Erith, Kent. As Assistant Chief Engineer in their laboratory, he was responsible for the design and development of ultra-high frequency (UHF) communication systems for air defence. He stayed with Burndept Limited for five years and during this time his eldest son and his daughter were born.

Rowley was elected as a member of the Institute of Radio Engineers in 1950.

Chapter 35
Establishing the KW Brand

In 1955, Rowley decided to set up his own company so that he could develop his own radio communication ideas. Initially he started out as 'Bristol Electronics' to carry out local TV and radio servicing and at the same time he was able to commence on design and manufacture of short-wave transmitters and receivers under the name of KW Electronics.

KW Electronics Limited was formally registered on the 6th January 1956, with Ruth as a Co-Director. Rowley's wartime colleague in Cairo, and old friend, Ken Ellis (G5KW) also joined the business. The name of the company was a logical derivation from his call sign (G8KW) and, at the start, he worked from a large shed (shack) and a garage in the back garden of the house in Wilmington, Kent. Early pieces of KW equipment have a metal ID plate which shows his Birchwood Road, Wilmington address. Ken later left the business to take up a senior communications role in Beirut, Lebanon.

In the 1950s many UK amateurs were using home-made or 'government surplus' equipment, which was readily available after the end of World War II. Rowley's company began to offer equipment which was specifically designed for radio amateurs, and this came either in kit-form or as a finished unit. The designs included transmitters, receivers and aerials. He also designed some commercial very-high-frequency (VHF) communications equipment and was pleased that four different models gained approvals from the British Post Office, which was still the controlling body for amateur licensing. He teamed up with companies such as Geloso from Italy, to use some of their components.

After a few years, KW Electronics had outgrown the home setting and, in 1960, Rowley found factory premises at Heath Street in nearby Dartford. This, he named 'Vanguard Works', following the theme used for one of his first major transmitters (KW Vanguard) which, in turn, had been inspired by his first post-war car – the silver 1950 Standard Vanguard Mark 1 saloon.

From the late 1950s onward 'KW kit' was widely advertised in electronics and amateur radio publications There were many different models produced over time and often these sets had names beginning with the letter 'V' such as Vanguard/Victor/Valiant/Vespa/Viceroy as well as KW brand labelling.

Within his new factory, Rowley was now able to increase production and grow the company by ploughing profits back into it. In the 1960s, KW Electronics continued to grow and won several Radio Society of Great Britain (RSGB) awards for manufacturing their equipment. The first of these awards was in 1960. One in 1962 was for the KW77 receiver, which was judged to be the best piece of manufactured equipment and another in 1963 was for the KW2000 transceiver. Each of these awards from the RSGB were presented to Rowley at international exhibitions in London. The KW2000 unit was possibly the first single side band transceiver for the radio amateur market and was exported to the United States and many other countries around the world. In 1963, an agreement was reached with an American company for these units to be manufactured and sold in the USA, South America and Mexico. Later, in 1965, it was discovered that the KW design for this product had been copied by a Japanese company. The original KW2000 unit was soon upgraded to the KW2000A and later, in 1969, to the very popular KW2000B. The last models were the KW2000D and KW2000E. Pictures showing the exhibition stand with the KW77 and Rowley proudly holding a KW2000 are shown in the photos section.

In 1962 the company had 30 employees and by 1965 it had grown further and now required more space for production and testing. An additional factory space (6,000 square feet) was found behind the High Street in nearby Crayford and was named 'Viceroy Works'. At this time KW Electronics was known as the leading British manufacturer of amateur radio equipment in Europe but mass produced (and cheaper) electronics from Japan were beginning to arrive in the UK. Rowley, and his design teams, had to really focus on costs in order to be competitive on price. KW was now employing around 100 people across all departments in the manufacturing process including its own Research and Development laboratory.

In 1967, Rowley negotiated a share exchange with Syd Wellum, on behalf of Delta Electronics of Toronto, Canada, and continued as Managing Director of the UK company. Syd was President of the Toronto company and became a lifelong friend.

Rowley travelled around the world forging new business links and his company expanded into design, development and production of transmitters and transceivers for the commercial market. Types of equipment supplied included high frequency and ultra-high frequency, long-range, base station and mobile radio communication systems, ground to air communications and navigation systems and broadcasting. Some of these systems required components from other companies. Much of the equipment they designed and built between 1966 and 1975 was produced for other communications companies such as Redifon (a large telecommunications company based in Wandsworth, London and part of the Rediffusion group) and Decca, who sold the equipment under their own branding. KW Electronics developed a close relationship with Redifon Ltd and undertook various sub-contract works with three major developments and production contracts for them. One of these was a large contract for over 500 VHF Radio Telephone (transceiver) units, for marine use. KW branded commercial equipment was also supplied to many overseas embassies, police forces and other Governmental organisations, as well as to Heathrow Airport.

Rowley was proud to advertise his KW branding on various vehicles he owned. He acquired the personalised car registration number plate 'KW 73', which was displayed on a Vauxhall Victor Estate in the 1960s. This was the chance combination of the KW call sign and company name and also the radio abbreviation of 73 which is used internationally by radio hams to send 'kind regards'. Rowley was disappointed that he was unable to transfer the registration to a subsequent vehicle as the Vauxhall estate had been registered as a 'commercial vehicle' to allow the transportation of company goods. However, some years later, he was able to acquire the registration '8 KW' which was held on an old Moped (later stolen from his factory) and this was much more personal to him. This time he was able to transfer the registration to several cars that he owned.

Medals awarded to Rowley, World War II service

Wilmington house - first base of KW Electronics in Kent, with Standard Vanguard in the drive

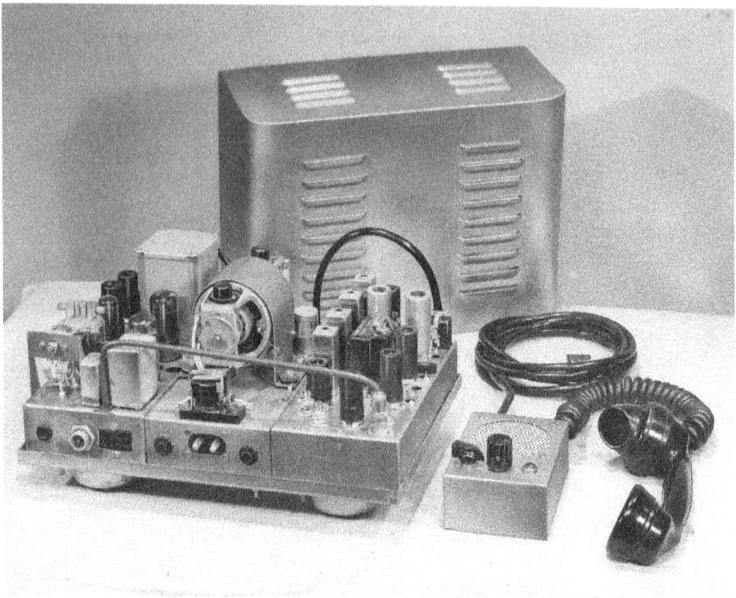

An early KW Radio Telephone from the 1950s

Rowley with 'KW Viceroy' transmitter

"The K.W. Vanguard"

Front Panel and Inside Appearance
(see over for Circuit)

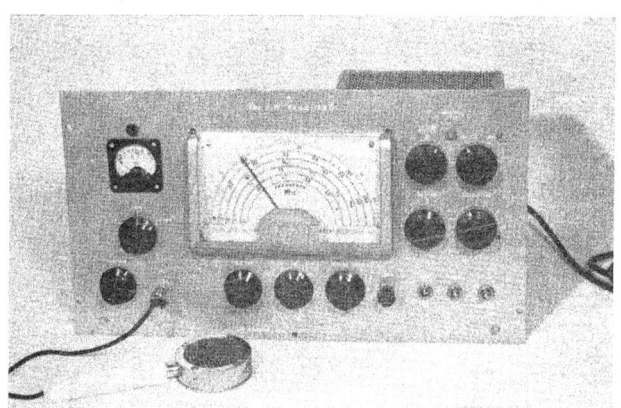

K. W. ELECTRONICS LTD.

Birchwood Road
G5KW   Wilmington   G8KW
Dartford, Kent, England.
(Swanley Junction 2137)

Promotional material for the 'KW Vanguard'. Reprinted from Short Wave Magazine, March 1958

Two photos of the KW Factory at Heath Street, Dartford, Kent, c1965

Radio Communications Exhibition Award for KW 77 Receiver, London 1962

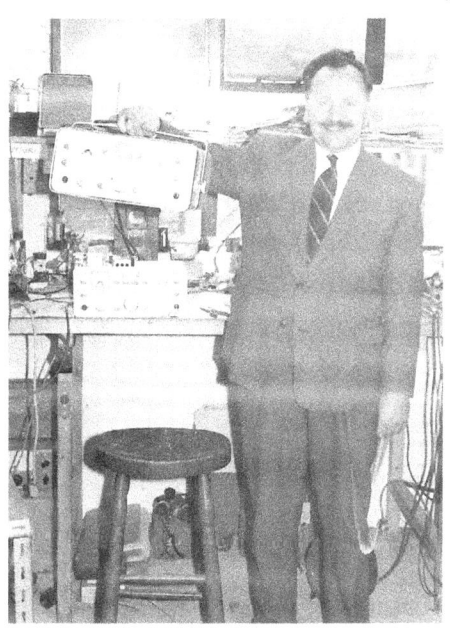

Rowley, in the KW factory, proudly showing an early KW 2000 transceiver

Rowley's G8KW / EA7GRM QSL card, 1987

Picture of Rowley with his Honary Membership certificate, in 2000, to commemorate the 50th anniversary of DARC

'G8KW Trophy' presented by Rowley to DARC for 50th anniversary in 2000

Chapter 36
Some Other KW Highlights

KW equipment plays a starring role

In *Dr No*, the first ever James Bond spy movie produced in 1962, radio equipment made by KW was featured and clearly showed the manufacturer's label from 'Dartford England'. The model used was the KW Vanguard, an AM transmitter, and it was hidden along with a receiver in a fake bookshelf. Actually, this was quite an achievement considering its physical size, but it looked convincing on screen!

Later, in 1969, one of Rowley's KW transceiver sets (KW2000A) was featured and pictured in the story line of the Peter O'Donnell strip cartoon called Modesty Blaise which appeared daily in the *London Evening Standard* newspaper from 1963 until around 2001.

Working with the Pirates – (Britain's Pirate Radio stations)

In the early 1960s, various pirate radio stations commenced broadcasting to the UK and became extremely popular. These stations were often based on ships, such as Radio Caroline and Radio London, and were anchored in the North Sea, just outside British waters. However, in the mid to late 1960s, the Government decided to close down these stations on the basis that they were causing interference with legitimate users and operators. In 1967 the Government passed the 1967 Marine Broadcasting Offences Act which made it an offence to broadcast from marine structures.

Rowley and KW Electronics Limited were approached to carry out work for the pirate radio stations, Britain Radio and Radio England and also Radio 390. Britain Radio and Radio England were on board the *MV Olga Patricia* in the North Sea off Frinton, Essex and Radio 390, described as an easy listening station, was operating from the, now semi-derelict WWII, Red Sands Fort in the Thames Estuary. Rowley enjoyed getting back into a music broadcasting environment and in 1965 the company supplied and installed the new transmitting equipment to the station. The medium-wave broadcast transmitter was powered by diesel generators and had an output of only 10kW feeding into a 50m vertical mast. Rowley sometimes travelled around the country taking signal strength readings and was quoted as saying that the signal coverage was much greater than expected.

Red Sands Fort was a former Maunsell fort (named after their designer, Guy Maunsell) built in the middle of the Thames estuary offshore from Whitstable in Kent. Originally, these seven steel-built tower structures were constructed locally in Gravesend before being towed downstream and then sunk into the Red Sands sandbar in 1943. The towers had housed anti-aircraft guns as well as living accommodation for Army personnel, and were there to defend shipping in the Thames and also London itself from the many Luftwaffe bombing attacks which regularly followed the route of the River Thames to reach the city.

It was on one of Rowley's visits to the Red Sands Fort in the mid 1960s that, as a teenager, I was allowed to join him one Sunday when the weather conditions were good. We joined a chartered fishing boat from Whitstable that was carrying various supplies to the fort and sailed out into the Thames. Arriving at the fort, we climbed up the massive access ladder and into one of the seven towers. There were five towers located around a sixth central one with the seventh being offset to one side. These were inter-connected by walkways some 100 feet above the sea. After seeing the Radio 390 studio, transmitting gear and 'mess' I was allowed a total free run of the towers! I recall it as feeling very eerie going up and down the different levels within some of the disused areas. There was even one occasion when I came down an internal staircase towards an open door expecting to see the walkway to the next tower only to find I wasn't on the walkway level and was looking straight down to the sea – no health and safety measures there! Fortunately, the trip ended safely and at the end of the afternoon we descended the ladder to the fishing boat and returned to land again. It was certainly a memorable experience!

In 1966, the management of Radio 390 were taken to court and found guilty of "Illegal Broadcasting" and, despite challenging the ruling, finally went off-air during 1967.

British Trans-Arctic Expedition (BTA)

In February 1968, when Sir Wally Herbert and his team set out with their dogs and sledges to cross the Arctic via the North pole, Rowley and a fellow radio amateur, Dennis Collins (G2FLB), were asked to support radio communications for Sir Wally's team and their Arctic base station back to the UK. Sir Wally's route across the Arctic took him from Point Barrow on the northern edge of Alaska to Spitzbergen via the North Pole. The direct journey was about 2000 miles but was expected to be up to 3800 miles, due to the shifting ice patterns.

Wally was the radio operator for the expedition team. To aid communications from Wally and the sledge team back to their base station, some 500 miles away, and then onto the UK expedition headquarters (based in London), a relay link was set up between the base station and the Royal Aircraft Establishment (RAE) at Farnborough. The RAE was not operational at weekends so Rowley, along with Dennis Collins, agreed to set up alternative links (using KW equipment) to the expedition base station, which they operated for every weekend of the 16-month expedition. A special licence was issued specifically for these communications (G7AE – 'AE' for Arctic Expedition) which gave Rowley and Dennis authority to operate at frequencies outside of the normal amateur radio frequency allocations.

Communications with the base station were in Morse, although unlike in his earlier wartime career, all messages were sent in plain English with no encoding. Using their KW amateur equipment,

Rowley and Dennis achieved a 95% contact success rate compared with 96.2% achieved by the RAE using commercial gear.

Following each contact with the base station, messages were then passed on by phone call immediately to Sir Miles Clifford, who was chairman of the BTA Expedition, and was based in London. Any messages to be sent back to the base team were telephoned to Rowley or Dennis.

Once the expedition team arrived back in Portsmouth, from Spitzbergen, Rowley was invited to a reception where he met Sir Wally and his team and was presented with a signed copy of his new book *Across the Top of the World* as a gesture of appreciation for Rowley's help during the expedition. He inscribed it with "To Rowley – with warmest thanks for all your help and encouragement". In his covering letter to Rowley, Sir Wally commented about his experience of writing and publishing his book and remarked "how much less stressful it is by comparison to cross the Arctic Ocean".

A Temporary End to the Original KW Brand and New Start-ups

In 1974, Rowley was approached by the Decca Group (at the time the group comprised two major British electronic/defence companies, Decca Navigator and Decca Radar as well as Decca Records) who wanted to get into the commercial communications business. The directors of KW Electronics (Rowley and Syd Wellum) decided to accept Decca's offer to purchase all KW assets, resulting in a new company called Decca Communications. The company moved from Dartford to a new base in Sevenoaks, Kent and Rowley was appointed as a director. Decca Communications continued to support both the amateur radio and commercial markets.

Sir Edward Lewis ran the Decca group, as Chairman, until a few days before his death in 1980, when it was sold to Racal. Racal decided that they did not wish to support the amateur market which meant that much of Rowley's original KW communications business was no longer relevant to them. They did, however, retain one product line (Decca Messenger transceivers) and moved it to one of their own factories. This gave Rowley the chance to buy back a large proportion of the KW/Decca assets and re-establish his original KW branding. The new company was called KW Communications Ltd. and Rowley established a new base in a factory (8,500 square feet) at Chatham.

Rowley formed another company in 1981, trading under the name KW Ten-Tec Ltd., to import and distribute Ten-Tec radio equipment. Ten-Tec were a quality manufacturer of amateur radio equipment in the USA. During this time there were also many commercial contracts undertaken in Nigeria and another company, KW Developments (Nigeria) Ltd., was set up. One such contract was to supply and install mobile communications to a large fleet of brand-new Honda 750 motorbikes for the Nigerian Police whilst another was to provide maintenance of airport communications systems. Unfortunately, this company had to close down in 1988 due to non-payment of many large-value invoices against the various contracts.

In the early 1990s, Rowley decided to sell the remainder of the KW Communications assets and to retire. He sold the business to a company called HRS Electronics Ltd.

Rowley was always very proud to have been a successful British manufacturer in communications during a challenging time when mass-produced units from the far east (mainly Japan) were starting to flood the market.

KW Remembered

Whilst the manufacture of the KW equipment ceased almost fifty years ago, KW still has a tremendous following and there are many collectors and clubs worldwide who regularly restore, rebuild and operate stations featuring KW transmitters, receivers and associated accessories. There is a continual market in second-hand KW equipment from the company and prices can often be more than the original purchase price. The National Radio Centre at Bletchley Park has a small collection of KW equipment which was originally housed in the RSGB museum at Potters Bar prior to its closure.

In the late 1990s, Dartford Council approved the name of 'Shears Close', off Oakfield Lane, for a new development built by a local firm, DBS Development Projects. The site was less than a mile from the Vanguard Works in Dartford and the name was in recognition of Rowley's contribution to employment and business in the area.

In 2016 the Cray Valley Radio Society organised the first 'KW Weekend' event in early January, as a celebration of KW Electronics. Since then, the event has been held every year on the weekend nearest to the incorporation date of the original limited company, which was on 6th January 1956. Other clubs and individual radio hams (worldwide, but mostly in the UK) are encouraged to participate. Each using different models of KW equipment, which have been lovingly restored and maintained over the years, the radio hams make contact with other radio hams worldwide, who are frequently also using KW equipment.

Some clubs and individuals apply for their own 'special event licence' to operate at this time. These licences usually incorporate 'KW' in their call signs; for example, GB8KW has been used by Cray Valley Radio Society.

As a licensed amateur since 1974, the author was delighted that he was allowed to take over his father's call sign, G8KW, in 2010 and has joined several of the KW Weekends at Cray Valley Radio Society.

Part V
OTHER MEMORIES OF MY FATHER

Chapter 37
Family Life and on the Airwaves

My father's love of all things radio and communications meant that he chose to follow this interest in both his work life and his spare time. Radio communications work, home projects, events and friendships were a key part of our family life when I was growing up.

From an early age, it was common to see him assembling equipment within our home. This included an early black and white television set, originally set up to watch the 1953 coronation of Queen Elizabeth II, and various amateur radios as well as audio equipment for home use. He passed that love of the radio world and music onto me as well as his practical electronics knowledge. Later on, he encouraged me to sit my radio amateurs exam.

When he was at home, but not working, (evenings, weekends and holidays) he prioritised his amateur radio hobby. He was regularly 'on the air' from the radio shack in his study and for many, many years he would keep a weekly Sunday contact, or 'sked' (schedule), with some of his friends around the world.

Many of the contacts he made through business or 'on the air' also became lifelong family friends. He was also able to meet many of them on his business and holiday trips to places such as Canada, Spain and Sweden as well as Germany.

My father remained lifelong friends with many of the German amateurs he got to know whilst in Hamburg. Every year DARC awards a glass trophy, known as 'The G8KW Trophy' for membership growth, training and youth work at local club level. (See photos section). The trophy was presented to DARC by 'Rowley KW' when he attended the 50th anniversary celebrations of the DARC, in 2000, at Friedrichshafen.

He held many radio licences (at differing times) in several countries, as well as those quoted earlier whilst he was in Germany; these were Spain, Canada, Nigeria, Cameroons, Malta, Kenya, Egypt and Greece as well as the KW Radio Club licence G4BKW.

The Malta licence came about because it was decided that we would take a family holiday there. My father did not want to be away from his amateur radio for more than a few days. Part of our checked baggage on that trip included a KW2000A transceiver and one of his KW long-wire (dipole) aerials. As part of his planning, he had applied for permission to temporarily import the equipment and obtain a Maltese amateur radio licence. He also got approval from the hotel (Mellieha Bay) to set up the aerial on their roof and run a cable to the guestroom we were staying in.

In the mid-1980s, my parents decided to take longer holidays and spend more time in Andalucia, Spain, settling on buying a small villa in an area where several of my father's expatriate friends already lived. Naturally, he wanted to operate his own radio station whilst spending time there. This, he set up in the spare bedroom and an aerial was installed on the roof terrace. He also applied for his Spanish amateur radio licence and was granted EA7GRM for use while in the country. My father, who still had a keen interest in languages, decided to learn Spanish in his mid-70s.

One other distinct memory I have of how my father's business life spilt over into our family life was that my wife and I had a Nigerian Chief (with one of his wives) at our wedding! This came about because on the week before our wedding, my father had been meeting with a Nigerian Chief who was visiting the UK. Business wasn't fully completed by the end of the week so the Chief suggested they should continue discussions on the next day, which was a Saturday. My father explained that this wouldn't be possible as his son was getting married that day. On hearing this, the Chief announced that he liked weddings and would come along too! So, much to the amusement and amazement of the families and the church minister, we had an interesting extra couple of guests at our wedding.

My father was appointed member of the Radio Club of America (est. 1908) in 1985 and in 1991, at a ceremony in New York, he was elevated to the rank of Fellow for services to the radio communications industry.

After a very full life, totally devoted to radio communications, my father sadly suffered the effects of Alzheimer's disease and passed away on 17th November 2009, aged 90 years. News of him as a silent key (SK), a term used by ham radio operators as a mark of respect for a deceased operator, quickly spread around the world. My mother survived him for a further two years and passed away on 27th January 2012.

Chapter 38
Postscript Regarding His War Years

Like many of his generation he did not talk much about his, once highly classified, work during WWII until much later in his life. In my father's case he had also been bound by the Official Secrets Act.

He wrote a couple of articles for local papers about small parts of his war experiences before finally starting to document the full story in the 1990s.

In 1999 he agreed to be interviewed for a Channel 4 television production called *The Spying Game*. He met the documentary team at Bletchley Park and later at his home. During the interview he recalled a few stories from his time working with SIME in the Middle East.

Since his death, more of his contacts in the amateur radio world have started to learn about my father's wartime exploits, mostly from talks given by my cousin, Colin, who had access to my father's handwritten notes about his life, after he died.

Untold stories of WWII are still emerging, and some individuals have belatedly been recognised for their achievements. My father's personal contribution undoubtedly contributed to the eventual Allied successes in WWII and he is probably one of the very few to have received the British Empire Medal as well as the Iron Cross!

- - - - - - - - E N D - - - - - - - -

Glossary

78 rpm records – flat discs for reproducing analogue audio with a rotational speed of 78 revolutions per minute (rpm). Often referred to as '78s'

'A' Force – created in Cairo in 1941 on Winston Churchill's direct orders as a highly secret division of Special Intelligence Service (MI6) for subterfuge and counterintelligence under the control of Colonel Dudley Wrangel Clarke (later Brigadier and OBE)

Abwehr – The German military intelligence service. Wilhelm Franz Canaris was its head, from 1935 to 1944

Aldis Lamp – A visual signalling device to transmit messages using Morse code

ATS – Auxiliary Territorial Service

Axis – The major countries in an alliance of Nazi Germany, Fascist Italy, and Japan

BAOR – British Army of the Rhine

BEF – British Expeditionary Force

BEM – The military British Empire Medal was awarded only to non-commissioned officers. It was awarded on 1,236 occasions during the whole of the second World War for gallant and distinguished service

Call Sign – A unique identifier for each amateur radio operator with the initial characters denoting the licensing country

C-in-C – Commander-in-Chief

CO – Commanding Officer. The officer in command of a complete military unit, often with rank of Lieutenant Colonel

Control Office for Germany and Austria – responsible for the management of the Control Commission for Germany and the Allied Commission for Austria

CSM – Company Sergeant Major

CSO – Chief Signals Officer

DARC – Deutscher Amateur Radio Club

DASD – Deutscher Amateur Sender Dienst (pre-war, German Amateur Transmitter Service)

DCSO – Deputy Chief Signals Officer

ENSA – Entertainments National Service Association

Force 133 – name of SOE headquarters in Cairo and responsible for operations across the Mediterranean, including Greece

GHQ – General Headquarters Middle East, based in Cairo, known as Grey Pillars

Grey Pillars – GHQ Middle East Command base, in Cairo, also referred to as The Secret Building

HMAS – His Majesty's Australian Ship

Kilocycles – Short for kilocycles per second (kc/s) in use at the time. Unit of frequency, denoting one thousand cycles per second. Now replaced by kilohertz, kHz

kW – abbreviation for kilowatts, unit of power

LRDG – Long Range Desert Group (reconnaissance and raiding unit of British Army)

Megacycles – Short for megacycles per second (mc/s) in use at the time. Unit of frequency, denoting one million cycles per second. Now replaced by megahertz, MHz

MEF – Middle East Forces

MI5 – The Security Service. During the War played a key role in uncovering enemy agents in Britain and providing misinformation back to Germany

MI6 – Secret Intelligence Service (SIS) which included 'A' Force Cairo

MO – Medical Officer

NCO – Non-commissioned officer

OC – Officer Commanding. Officer (often rank of captain or major) in command of a sub-unit, within a main unit which would be commanded by a CO

OCTU – Officers Cadet Training Unit

Operation Mincemeat – huge deception plan with fake Allied invasion plans found on corpse (British Soldier, Major William Martin, who never actually existed) recovered in Spain and possibly found their way to Hitler's desk

OM – literally 'old man', a friendly greeting for an amateur radio operator

Polygon – Polygon Wireless Station (PWS)

PWS – Polygon Wireless Station (Abbassieh Garrison, on the outskirts of Cairo). The wireless station for GHQ

Q Code – 3-letter groups of abbreviations used in radio messages as a shortened form of communication to save time and ease communications. All beginning with letter Q

QSO – Q code abbreviation for 'a contact' or communication

Python Scheme – codename for prioritising return of troops that had served over four years overseas to come back to the UK

Radio Ham – A licensed amateur radio operator

RARO – Regular Army Reserve of Officers

Glossary

RMS – Royal Mail Ship (i.e. Mauretania)

Royal Corps of Signals – given its Royal Warrant by Winston Churchill on 28th June 1920 and confirmed by King George V six weeks later

RSGB – Radio Society of Great Britain

RSS – Radio Security Service, headquartered at Arkley View near Barnet

SAS – Special Air Service, founded in 1941

SK – Silent key (used to denote a deceased radio operator)

SIME – Security Intelligence Middle East. Security and counter-intelligence in the area under command of GHQ

SIS – Secret Intelligence Service (MI6)

SOE – Special Operations Executive, formed in 1940

SS – German "Schutzstaffel". The literal translation is 'protection squadron'. The German elite guard/paramilitary of the Nazi Party

STC – Standard Telephones and Cables, a British telephone, radio and telecommunications manufacturer

Tannoy – common name for a public address messaging system. Tannoy was the name of a company manufacturing public address equipment which then became commonly used as a verb and a noun

TD – Territorial Decoration (for Military long service)

VI's – Voluntary interceptors, organised in groups within RSS

WOSB – War Office Selection Board

XX – Roman numeral for Twenty – could also stand for Double Cross. From 1941 'The Twenty Committee' co-ordinated (dis)information and managed double agents

www.ingramcontent.com/pod-product-compliance
Lightning Source LLC
Chambersburg PA
CBHW050029090426
42735CB00021B/3427